CURRICULUM WORK AS
PUBLIC MORAL ENT

CURRICULUM WORK AS A PUBLIC MORAL ENTERPRISE

EDITED BY
RUBÉN A. GAZTAMBIDE-FERNÁNDEZ
AND JAMES T. SEARS

ROWMAN & LITTLEFIELD PUBLISHERS, INC.
Lanham • Boulder • New York • Toronto • Oxford

ROWMAN & LITTLEFIELD PUBLISHERS, INC.
Published in the United States of America
by Rowman & Littlefield Publishers, Inc.
A wholly owned subsidiary of The Rowman & Littlefield Publishing Group, Inc.
4501 Forbes Boulevard, Suite 200, Lanham, Maryland 20706
www.rowmanlittlefield.com

P. O. Box 317, Oxford OX2 9RU, UK

British Library Cataloguing in Publication Information Available

Library of Congress Cataloging-in-Publication Data

Curriculum work as a public moral enterprise / edited by Rubén A.
Gaztambide-Fernández and James T. Sears.
    p. cm.
Includes bibliographical references and index.
  ISBN 0-7425-2639-9 (cloth : alk. paper) — ISBN 0-7425-2640-2 (paper :
alk. paper)
  1. Critical pedagogy. 2. Curriculum planning—Philosophy. I.
Gaztambide-Fernández, Rubén A., 1971– II. Sears, James T. (James
Thomas), 1951–
  LC196 .C87 2004
  375'.001—dc22

                        2003019852

Printed in the United States of America

∞™ The paper used in this publication meets the minimum requirements of American
National Standard for Information Sciences—Permanence of Paper for Printed Library
Materials, ANSI/NISO Z39.48-1992.

CONTENTS

Introduction

RUBÉN A. GAZTAMBIDE-FERNÁNDEZ, HARVARD GRADUATE
SCHOOL OF EDUCATION

*The mode of being of the new intellectual can no longer consist in elo-
quence, which is an exterior and momentary mover of feelings and passions, but in active participation in practical life, as constructor, organiser,
"permanent persuader" and not just a simple orator.*

—GRAMSCI (1971, 10)

*When they are remote from the popular masses and interact only with
their books, intellectuals run the risk of arriving at a rarified
rationality, a disembodied understanding of the world.*

—FREIRE AND FAUNDEZ (1998, 215)

Italian Marxist scholar and political organizer Antonio Gramsci and
Brazilian philosopher and educator Paulo Freire are two of the most often cited scholars in contemporary curriculum theory. Their works have
had a major influence in contemporary thinking about culture, pedagogy, and
power (Araújo Freire and Macedo 1998; Borg, Buttigieg, and Mayo 2002;
Gaztambide-Fernández, Harding, and Sordé-Martí 2004; Mayo 1999).
Gramsci's concept of hegemony and his deep thinking into matters of culture and cultural change have been central to the radical rethinking of curriculum work.[1] While Freire's work was more intently focused on education,
particularly his theorizing about matters of pedagogy, emancipation, and his
concept of *conscientização*,[2] his ideas have been influential worldwide (Araújo

Freire and Macedo 1998) and have extended beyond education into community organizing and forms of action research.[3]

In addition to their theoretical and intellectual contributions, Gramsci and Freire had a deep commitment to and extensive experience in practice—organizing and working with groups in political struggles and teaching a wide range of groups in a variety of settings. Before spending most of his adult life as a political prisoner, for example, Gramsci was a leader of the Italian Communist Party and a member of the Italian Parliament. Through his political career, Gramsci stressed the importance of grassroots organizing and the education of the working class through political struggles. He also wrote extensively for newspapers and magazines on matters of art, culture, and political organization. Like Gramsci, Freire's intellectual contributions emerge directly from his experiences and direct participation in political and educational projects. Freire was a teacher of adult learners, served as secretary of education in Brazil, and traveled the world assisting former colonies in literacy campaigns. Gramsci and Freire were, in the complete sense of the term, public intellectuals. Their theoretical work was embedded and directly informed by their actions and their commitments; both engaged publicly in popular struggles.

Curriculum scholars, particularly since the "reconceptualization," have been accused of taking distance from the practical and public dimensions of curriculum work (Hlebowitz 1993; Jackson 1980; Sears 1992; Wraga 1999). It may be true that the work of curriculum scholars in the past thirty years has remained somewhat distant from the hands of teachers and educators working in schools and other learning communities. However, as William F. Pinar argues in chapter 11, it is not true that this distance was chosen or by any means desired. In his concluding chapter to this volume, Pinar argues that this was a forced distance, provoked by the political backlash on progressive education and the turn to positivistic and technical views of teaching and learning—a backlash with plenty of precedence in the educational history of the United States (Marshall et al. 2004).

Furthermore, it is also questionable whether curriculum scholars have been removed altogether from the practice of teaching. In fact, the intellectual work of curriculum scholars cannot be detached from their work as teachers and mentors not only of young scholars but also of preservice teachers and other educators who have pursued advanced studies in education and educational theory (Schubert et al. 1988). Curriculum theorists have never stopped teaching, save the sporadic sabbatical, and, as some of their autobiographical reflections suggest, their academic careers are continuations of earlier teaching experiences (such as Schubert 1992). In this sense, I would argue that curriculum scholars are—to borrow loosely a Gramscian concept—*organic* to the teaching profession.[4] While historical, social, and political forces may have tipped the social role of these intellectuals toward a more distant (Gramsci may have called it *traditional*) relationship with the teaching profession, many curriculum scholars have been committed to developing sophisticated theories of curriculum that embrace rather than elide its foundation in educational practice and thought. As Pinar argues in chapter 11, the distance between curriculum theorizing and educational practice has not been fundamentally a problem of methodological distance but a problem of the conditions under which curriculum work must occur.

As James T. Sears aptly demonstrates in chapter 1, this distance between scholarly work and practice is relatively recent. He gives many examples of scholars at the turn and during the first half of the twentieth century whose conceptual and theoretical work was directly related to their role in the public sphere. Admitting that his and others' earlier criticism of contemporary curriculum theory should have been "tempered with greater historical insight, practical patience, and intellectual humility" (4), Sears argues in his chapter that the turn of the twenty-first century is a turning point in the relationship between "theorists" and "practitioners" as curriculum workers in universities and school districts continue to bridge the distance between their thoughts and their actions toward a more unitary and collaborative praxis.

For Freire (1970), praxis implied a balance between thinking and doing and a close imbricate relationship between the two:

> Within the word we find two dimensions, reflection and action, in such radical interaction that if one is sacrificed—even in part—the other immediately suffers. . . . When a word is deprived of its dimension of action, reflection automatically suffers as well, and the word is changed into idle chatter, into *verbalism*, into an alienated and alienating "blah." It becomes an empty word, one which cannot denounce the world, for denunciation is impossible without a commitment to transform, and there is not transformation without action. (75–76)

Both Freire and Gramsci point out that intellectual activity is not just the purview of some, but that all individuals engage in forms of intellectual activity because all activity involves some kind of "intellectual-cerebral elaboration," to use Gramsci's (1971) words. This is not to say, as Gramsci carefully argues, that all persons "have in society the function of intellectuals" (9). Instead, they argue that a direct correlation between thought and action and between intellectuals and the social group(s) to which they correspond is essential for the kind of fundamental social transformation that radical curriculum scholars envision.

In the spring of 2001, I was a student in Sears's curriculum theory course at the Harvard Graduate School of Education, where he was a visiting professor. About a dozen students with a wide range of backgrounds and interests joined that class and engaged in collective readings and discussions of classic texts, such as Ralph Tyler's (1949) *Basic Principles of Curriculum and Instruction* and Pinar's (2000b) *Curriculum Studies: The Reconceptualization.* While each student took a different approach to research directed by individual interests, we were all concerned with the challenges of making coherent theory/practice connections and understanding the relationship between the work of theorists and that of practitioners. Our own "complicated conversation" about curriculum was informed by conversations with curriculum scholars such as Janet Miller, J. Dan Marshall, Patti Lather, and Peter Hlebowitz. We asked what they thought ought to be their role in, and how they saw their scholarship contributing to, the development of a rigorous and sophisticated public debate about education.

The responses of these scholars to our queries made it clear, at least to Jim and me, that their current work and the preoccupations and insights of the students in the class pointed to another turn in curriculum scholarship, one that underscored the relationship between theory and practice.[5] It occurred to us that it was important to produce a collection of chapters that documented this current turn in curriculum work. It quickly became evident that in order to serve its purpose, our project, by definition, could not reflect the traditional form of scholars and academics reflecting on the status of the field. Instead, we wanted to bring together the voices of curriculum theorists working within academic settings and practitioners working in schools and other educational settings to document their *collaborative* work and to present it in a way that was useful to practitioners and academics alike. In form and in content, this collection of chapters represents a shift in curriculum work practice and scholarship. In form, *Curriculum Work as a Public Moral Enterprise* challenges the assumption that practitioners are supposed to be only consumers of theory and that academics are expected to produce independent scholarly work. In content, this book engages readers in the complicated conversation about the relationship between theory and practice, between theoreticians and practitioners.

Each chapter documents a collaboration between theorists and practitioners. Although every author is, to some degree, a practitioner as well as a theorist, their collaborative work emerges from the particular positions and identifications that each assumed in his or her respective efforts in praxis. From working with homeless youth to deepening one's personal commitment to antiracist pedagogy in schools, each chapter implodes the false binary of the theory/practice dichotomy, illuminating a different dimension of the challenges therein.

Together, the chapters in this book articulate three challenges in the current turn in curriculum work: discursive, structural, and personal. While each chapter, to some extent, touches on all three, contributors offer insights about some challenges more than others. The discursive challenge is characterized by the need to change the terms of debate and the rhetoric associated with public discussions about education. The ways in which we think and speak about a problem determine the range of possible solutions. "Discursive practices," noted philosopher Michel Foucault (1977), "are embodied in technical processes, in institutions, in patterns for general behavior, in forms for transmission and diffusion, and in pedagogical forms which, at once, impose and maintain them" (199).

In chapter 2, Joanne M. Arhar and Rebecca McElfresh, a university-based and a K–12 educator respectively, eloquently discuss the rhetoric in contemporary curriculum work. They argue that the different assumptions that curriculum workers make about the nature of teaching and learning and about the goals of public schooling (analyzed in terms of contrasting ideologies) are a crucial source of tension in public debate. They suggest that there are internal contradictions in the dominant technical-rational view of schooling, suggesting that the theory/practice gap is not just one of professional position but an actual gap between what is said and thought and what is done. Exposing this gap, particularly in the rhetoric of standards-based reform and the positivist clamor for replicable and experimental research, Arhar and McElfresh suggest that "moving beyond the talk of educational reform to what matters most to teachers (that is, the disciplines) may help problematize and deconstruct current practice, illuminating the ways in which our current configurations inhibit new vision" (25).

My colleague Anne R. Clark, a high school teacher, and I, a university-based researcher, present a related argument in chapter 5. Shifting the way we talk and think about the arts and their relationship to academics, we suggest, is fundamental to constructing a viable vision for the role of arts high schools in U.S. culture. We argue that at the heart of the current challenge in arts education is an unnecessary discursive distinction between arts and academics. By rethinking this relationship, we not only address public expectations about the role of the artist in society but also satisfy the demands of public education. Again, it is through shifting the discursive regimes that we construct a reconceptualized curriculum.

The structural challenge of contemporary curriculum work is, perhaps, most evident in this book. For instance, working across academic and school boundaries requires crossing physical structures as well as geographic boundaries. It also requires negotiating time structures and the hierarchies of various positions, the expectations of our structured work environments, and our prescribed career paths.

In chapter 3, Barbara Brodhagen, a longtime teacher and school practitioner, and Michael W. Apple, a well-known curriculum theorist, describe how they and their students come together in the space of a public school classroom and how these interactions inform their work. They suggest ways of shortening the physical distance between schoolwork and academic reflection. At the heart of their chapter is the essence of collaboration between school practitioner and university scholars as graduate students and university professors enter a public classroom to engage in a conversation about economic forces and the impact of globalization on communities around the world. The lessons for the high school students and teachers as well as for the university-based students and professors are immeasurable and are attainable, according to the authors, only through this kind of direct contact and dialogic exchange across and within the structural boundaries of schools and universities.

The trans-Pacific collaboration between Mina Kim and Soo Ryeon Lee, documented in chapter 4, also highlights the structural dimensions of approaching curriculum work as a public moral enterprise. Most evidently, the physical distance of the two authors presents a clear challenge. But at a deeper level, the challenges of time allocation, state-mandated curriculum, lack of experience with a particular subject, and the structure of the existing curriculum become the fundamental structural challenges that Kim and Lee must address. The success of their effort to develop an early childhood curriculum for Korean unification speaks to the potential rewards and importance of creative thinking in facing such structural challenges. This is especially so as curriculum scholars seek to *internationalize* their work, a "move [that] is crucially important politically and ethically" (Trueit 2003, xiii).[6]

The work of developing "transformative curriculum leadership," as described by Rosemary Gornik, James Henderson, and Michelle D. Thomas in chapter 6, also points to the structural challenges of constructing curriculum as public intellectuals. The authors were fortunate to work in a school with a proven record of excellence (within the dominant discourse of high standards), allowing them freedom to explore an alternative approach to curriculum. Nonetheless, and despite their hard-earned success with participants, the demands of existing professional structures and the lack of financial support were unexpectedly difficult barriers, requiring "an internal change process" (59). They ask, "How can school leaders work collaboratively with teachers to maintain an interconnectedness of high standards, sophisticated decision making, ongoing professional inquiry, and student learning while embracing transformative practices?" (59).

Because the work of praxis is rooted in an embodied knowing of the world, personal investments are required, and the willingness to put oneself at risk is necessary; embracing our role as public intellectuals means knowing that what we think can never be separated from who we are. Clearly this is not always easy, as Morna McDermott, Toby Daspit, and Kevin Dodd illustrate in chapter 7. They articulate the need to be risk takers, recognizing that such actions often lead not to the anticipated outcomes but rather to the unexpected and at times the unwanted. Using Augusto Boal's *Theatre of the Oppressed* (Boal 1985) methodology with teachers, the authors hoped "to improve course content and develop both teaching strategies and evaluation methods that enhance the discussion of multicultural issues through theatrical methods" (83). Despite their eagerness and early positive response and their new and invigorating new discourse, they faced structural challenges, encountered hesitation, and ultimately resistance.

Through "taking teachers to the streets," Susan Finley and Jason Adams develop in chapter 8 a theory of teaching and learning rooted in personal experiences. Based on their knowledge and commitment to the education of homeless youth, coupled with their experiences with the arts, professor and student reflect on their learning as an "act of becoming." Having experienced firsthand exclusion from the structures of social order and thoughtfully developing an artistic language of their own, Finley and Adams move with ease into a space of personal connection with, commitment to, and support for each other. Their personal connection carries their work with homeless youth, emerging with a deeper and more personal understanding of what it means to teach and to learn.

The personal and autobiographical dimensions of curriculum work are also explicit in chapter 9, by Nina Asher and Michelle Haj-Broussard. In true dialog form, they explore the personal challenges of moving into the "complicated conversation" of curriculum work, complicated further by the desire to make this conversation *practical*. This intellectual work, they argue, demands personal sacrifices, including being in the dangerous interstices of identity construction with their students as they interrogate the structures and the discursive regimes that appear so commonsensical. In their exchange, the authors offer profound insights about the internal processes of curriculum work as a public moral enterprise.

In every instance, the work of these curriculum workers has relied, ultimately, on their collaborative relationship. Such collaborations are not guarantors of success but do yield important lessons. Following Freire (1970), it is in the totality of their collaborative work that these authors contribute to the transformation of curriculum work into a public moral enterprise:

> [W]hile to say the true word—which is work, which is praxis—is to transform the world, saying that word is not the privilege of some few men [and women], but the right of every man [and woman]. Consequently, no one can say a true word alone—nor can he [or she] say it for another. (76)

This "contemporary praxis of collaboration," as described by Marilyn Doerr and J. Dan Marshall in chapter 10, requires envisioning new ways of working together. Drawing on her experiences as a teacher of ecology and environmental science, Doerr constructs a pedagogical and empirical project based on Pinar's (2000a) concept of *currere*. She makes explicit the collaborative dimensions of her work, which evolves into "environmental autobiography." This collaboration is neither straightforward nor obvious but involves a complex set of events, discoveries, and exchange characteristic of the postmodern digital world.

When understood in the context of the three challenges outlined in this introduction, the idea of collaboration is problematic. It assumes somewhat stable differences between the parties collaborating. Collaborating relies on distinctions between the functions and roles that the parties assume. For instance, when Apple and his students enter Brodhagen's classroom, their expert authority sets the collaborative stage, which is defined by such structural distinctions as high school and university and the discursive distinction between "white" (local) students and "Other" (international) students. While these a priori distinctions define the collaborative effort, it is the personal willingness to transgress such boundaries that makes the effort part of a radical turn in curriculum work.

While such situations have the potential to exacerbate rather than ameliorate the very structural, discursive, and personal distinctions that the anticipated turn in curriculum theory seeks to challenge, the distinctions embedded in the *idea* of collaboration are not necessary in practice. They simply define the conditions (and perhaps some degree of certainty) under which radical curriculum collaboration begins and the challenges it must face to, in the words of George S. Counts (1932), "build a new social order." Yet, as Counts put it, "society is never redeemed without effort, struggle, and sacrifice" (4). Both Freire and Gramsci dedicated their lives to the precarious interstice between their roles as intellectuals, educators, and political revolutionaries. Curriculum collaborators, as "public moral intellectuals," must challenge the *structural* boundaries imposed by the *discursive* regimes that shape how we *personally* proceed in an educational world not of our choice or desire. To fulfill our roles as curriculum workers, we must be willing to make personal sacrifices and to leap into the "complicated conversation" of curriculum work as a public moral enterprise. In the end, as Doerr and Marshall eloquently state,

> When [collaboration] works, none of us loses our identity, our autonomy. And at the same time, we become better, we become more. In our contemporary praxis of collaboration, the whole is truly greater than the sum of its parts. (118)

Notes

1. Ironically, conservative thinkers such as Harold Entwistle (1989) and E. D. Hirsch Jr. (1996) have also drawn on Gramsci's work, specifically his writings about education, to support conservative approaches to curriculum. For a careful critique of their analyses of Gramsci, see Giroux (2000, chap. 4).

2. *Conscientização* can be loosely translated into English as "conscientization," and it describes a process of becoming conscious of one's social positions and the political dimensions of being in the world. For more on this concept, see Freire (1970).

3. See, for example, the work of de los Reyes and Gozemba (2002), particularly their chapter on Helen Lewis and Highlander. See also Lather (1986, 1991) and the edited collection by Reason and Bradbury (2001).

4. It would be theoretically inaccurate to describe teachers as a social class in the sense that Gramsci uses to describe organic intellectuals. Nonetheless, I believe that his concept is useful here.

5. See chapter 1 in this volume and Marshall et al. (2004) for what they describe as other "turning points" in curriculum work.

6. The establishment of the International Association for the Advancement of Curriculum Studies and the ongoing work of curriculum scholars around the world to establish a worldwide field of curriculum studies has been an important new direction in this area. See the essays in Pinar (2003) and Trueit et al. (2003).

References

Araújo Freire, A. M., and D. Macedo. 1998. Introduction. In *The Paulo Freire reader*, edited by A. M. Araújo Freire and D. Macedo. New York: Continuum, 1–44.

Boal, A. 1985. *Theatre of the oppressed.* Translated by C. McBride and M. McBride. New York: Theatre Communications Group.

Borg, C., J. Buttigieg, and P. Mayo, eds. 2002. *Gramsci and education.* Lanham, Md.: Rowman & Littlefield.

Counts, G. S. 1932. *Dare the school build a new social order?* New York: Stratford Press.

de los Reyes, E., and P. Gozemba. 2002. *Pockets of hope.* Westport, Conn.: Bergin & Garvey.

Entwistle, H. 1989. *Antonio Gramsci: Conservative schooling for radical politics.* Boston: Routledge & Kegan Paul.

Foucault, M. 1977. *Language, counter-memory, practice: Selected essays and interviews by Michel Foucault.* Translated by D. F. Bouchard and S. Simon. Ithaca, N.Y.: Cornell University Press.

Freire, P. 1970. *Pedagogy of the oppressed.* New York: Continuum.

Freire, P., and A. Faundez. 1998. Learning to question: A pedagogy of liberation. In *The Paulo Freire reader*, edited by A. M. Araújo Freire and D. Macedo. New York: Continuum, 186–230.

Gaztambide-Fernández, R. A., H. Harding, and T. Sordé-Martí, eds. 2004. *Cultural studies and education: Perspectives on theory, methodology, and practice*. Cambridge, Mass.: Harvard Educational Review.

Giroux, H. A. 2000. *Stealing innocence: Corporate culture's war on children*. New York: Palgrave.

Gramsci, A. 1971. *Selections from the prison notebooks*. Translated by Q. Hoare and G. N. Smith. New York: International Publishers.

Hirsch, E. D., Jr. 1996. *The schools we need*. New York: Doubleday.

Hlebowitz, P. S. 1993. *Radical curriculum theory reconsidered: A historical approach*. New York: Teachers College Press.

Jackson, P. 1980. Curriculum and its discontents. *Curriculum Inquiry* 10(1): 28–43.

Lather, P. 1986. Research as praxis. *Harvard Educational Review* 56(2): 150–71.

———. 1991. *Getting smart: Feminist research and pedagogy with/in the postmodern*. New York: Routledge.

Marshall, J. D., J. T. Sears, W. H. Schubert, L. Allen, and P. Roberts. 2004. *Turning points in curriculum: A contemporary American memoir*. 2nd ed. Upper Saddle River, N.J.: Merrill/Prentice Hall.

Mayo, P. 1999. *Gramsci, Freire, and adult education: Possibilities for transformative action*. New York: Zed Books.

Pinar, W. 2000a. *Currere*: Towards reconceptualization. In *Curriculum studies: The reconceptualization*, edited by W. Pinar. Troy, N.Y.: Educators International Press, 396–414.

———, ed. 2000b. *Curriculum studies: The reconceptualization*. Troy, N.Y.: Educators International Press.

———, ed. 2003. *International handbook of curriculum research*. Mahwah, N.J.: Lawrence Erlbaum Associates.

Reason, P., and H. Bradbury, eds. 2001. *Handbook of action research: Participative inquiry and practice*. London: Sage.

Schubert, W. H. 1992. Practitioners influence curriculum theory: Autobiographical reflections. *Theory into Practice* 31(3): 236–43.

Schubert, W. H., A. L. Lopez-Schubert, L. Herzog, G. Posner, and C. Kridel. 1988. A genealogy of curriculum researchers. *Journal of Curriculum Theorizing* 38(2): 137–84.

Sears, J. 1992. The second wave of curriculum theorizing: Labyrinths, orthodoxies, and other legacies of the glass bead game. *Theory into Practice* 31(3): 210–18.

Trueit, D. 2003. Preface: Democracy and conversation. In *The internationalization of curriculum studies*, edited by D. Trueit, W. Doll Jr., H. Wang, and W. Pinar. New York: Peter Lang, ix–xvii.

Trueit, D., W. Doll Jr., H. Wang, and W. Pinar, eds. 2003. *The internationalization of curriculum studies*. New York: Peter Lang.

Tyler, R. W. 1949. *Basic principles of curriculum and instruction*. Chicago: University of Chicago Press.

Wraga, W. G. 1999. Extracting sun-beams out of cucumbers: The retreat from practice of reconceptualized curriculum studies. *Educational Researcher* 28: 4–13.

The Curriculum Worker as Public Moral Intellectual

I

JAMES T. SEARS, INDEPENDENT SCHOLAR

How can you have a career and never say anything?

—ABBEY LINCOLN, JAZZ SINGER

Since Joseph Schwab (1969) declared the curriculum field moribund, and following its reconceptualization there has been a distancing between curriculum theory and curriculum development. Paradoxically, as the curriculum field enjoyed a discursive renaissance, progressive bridges between school practitioners and curriculum scholars were all but washed away. In this chapter, I briefly describe this legacy of collaborative curriculum making and the role of the curriculum worker as a public moral intellectual.

The Rise and Fall of the Progressive Curriculum Worker

> [A]s more curriculum writing moves away from the field's once-singular emphasis on curriculum development, its long-standing identity as an institutionalized field with its own canon has floundered, shaped as it was by its association with schooling. (Sears and Marshall 2000, 210)

My use of the phrase "curriculum worker" is purposeful. It conveys the essential hands-on collaborative legacy of our field that intertwines progressive curriculum thought with educational and social reform: from Francis Wayland Parker's work in Quincy, Massachusetts, and Chicago and his nationally known *Talks on Pedagogics* (1894) to Alice and John Dewey's work in their Chicago laboratory school and the latter's seminal writings; from the curriculum development activity of Carlton Washburne in nearby Winnetka to Hollis Caswell's leadership at Teachers College's Horace Mann–Lincoln School Institute of School Experimentation and his synoptic *Curriculum Development* (Caswell and Campbell 1935); from Horace Mann Bond's curriculum development activities as an administrator at Dillard, Lincoln, and Atlanta Universities along with his scholarship on African American education (Bond 1934, 1939) to the groundbreaking work of Ida B. Wells and Mary McCleod Bethune; and from Ralph Tyler's leadership in evaluating the experimental schools, later known as the Eight-Year Study (Smith and Tyler 1942) and his influential *Basic Principles of Curriculum and Instruction* (1949) to the progressive curriculum work of Florence Stratemeyer (1931; Stratemeyer, Forkner, and McKim 1947), Laura Zirbes (1935), J. Galen Saylor (1941), Alice Miel (1946), and Harold Alberty (1947).

Twining curriculum thought with school practice was also evident in projects ranging from Harold Rugg's elementary social studies series (1929–1932) *Man and His Changing Society* and his teacher-friendly journal *The Social Frontier* to the curriculum efforts led by Superintendent Jesse Newlon in Denver. It, too, was apparent in eddies of innovation, such as the School for Organic Growth in Fairhope, Alabama, and the radicalism of adult education at Highlander, Commonwealth, Black Mountain, Berea, and Goddard (Lobdell 1984; Sears 1985). Such reform efforts dotted the rural landscape like newly painted barns hustling tobacco and Burma Shave signs posted along two-lane highways.

These and many other progressive efforts and visionaries, aptly detailed by others (such as Cremin 1961; Kliebard 1986; Schubert 1986; Schubert et al. 2002; Tanner and Tanner 1995; Urban 1992), contoured a conversation around the public moral dimensions of curriculum work. They opposed the rising tides of nationalism and xenophobia, scientific management and social efficiency, intolerance and bigotry, educational and social inequalities.

Although proponents such as Hilda Taba (1950) and Stephen Corey (1953) continued to be visible, collaborative curriculum making declined with the onset of World War II. During the Cold War era, progressives were assaulted, and their work was undermined by neoconservatives (such as Bestor 1953; Flesch 1955), the rapid consolidation of school districts, the exponential expansion of higher education, the passage of the National Education Defense Act, and the Woods Hole Conference the following year, 1959. It was a turning point in the field (Marshall, Sears, and Schubert 2000).

By the 1960s, the field of curriculum development—defined by educational professors working collaboratively with rank-and-file teachers and administrators—had all but disappeared from the post-*Sputnik* landscape. The production of "teacherproof" curriculum and disciplined-based projects such as MACOS (Man: A Course of Study) and BSCS (Biological Sciences Curriculum Study); the publication of books such as *Preparing Instructional Objectives* (Mager 1962); a curriculum discourse informed by the psychological language of cognition, development, and behavior; and curricula developed by discipline specialists, funded through foundations, and empowered by federal legislation replaced the cottage industry of collaborative curriculum development. As curriculum development became the province of others, most curriculum professors cowered in professional academic organizations and retired to the greenery of academia. Although a few "muted heretics," such as Hilda Taba (1962), Paul Klohr (1967), Theodore Brameld (1965), and Wells Foshay (McNally and Passow 1960), persevered in collaborative curriculum work, rational curriculum making was the norm (Marshall et al. 2000; Schubert et al. 2002).

From these curriculum malcontents working within the maelstrom of social discontent, a new generation of *curricularists* emerged. Within a decade, groundbreaking books, including *Curriculum Theorizing: The Reconceptualists* (Pinar 1975), *Ideology and Curriculum* (Apple 1979), *The Educational Imagination* (Eisner 1979), and *Landscapes of Learning* (Greene 1978), evidenced a renaissance of curriculum thought. For many curriculum scholars schooled into that generation, the "second wave" (Pinar 1988) of curriculum work within schools and with school practitioners was to be a dream deferred—something "dreamt into existence by others" (Pinar 1992). Curriculum professors watered at the American Educational Research Association with its newly created Special Interest Groups and retreated to small niche conferences. Once the hub of professorial and practitioner connections, many professors abandoned the Association for Supervision and Curriculum Development as it corporatized, selling its progressive soul for an ever-expanding membership (and commercial) base and Greater Washington Beltway influence.

In the process, "our curriculum conversation underwent a dramatic shift away from curriculum as a field in direct service to the institution of schooling toward one committed to understanding itself" (Marshall, Sears, and Adair 2001, 30). In nightmarish fashion, wave upon wave of statewide testing, district-mandated standards, and legislated teacher accountability washed away classrooms of joy, creativity, and critical thinking. Voices for affirmative action and nonsectarian education were drowned out against a dispiriting sea of right-wing legal briefs and stealth school board candidates while public schools were racially resegregated and variegated along class lines.

Some curriculum scholars were impatient with the apparent disconnect between cutting-edge concepts and everyday school experience (such as Ellsworth 1989; Jackson 1979; Sears 1992). In retrospect, these criticisms could have been tempered with greater historical insight, practical patience, and intellectual humility, as the intellectual work of curriculum trailblazers (such as Pinar 1974b, 1975; Pinar and Grumet 1976) would be appropriated by school workers a generation later. Meanwhile, others embarked in collaborative projects that encompassed "personal practical knowledge" of teachers (Clandinin and Connelly 1987, 1988, 1992), teacher lore (Schubert 1989, 1991; Schubert and Ayers 1992; Schubert and Lopez-Schubert 1982), and teacher lives and voices (Duckworth 1986, 1987; Goodson 1992; Miller 1990a, 1990b).

As in the first decades of the twentieth century, the United States is undergoing a profound geopolitical, technological, and cultural transformation. From robber baron J. D. Rockefeller and the Standard Oil Trust to Bill Gates and Microsoft; from the business-first presidential administrations of Harding and Coolidge to those of Reagan and the first and second Bushes; from Teapot Dome to Enron; from Attorney General A. Mitchell Palmer and the Red Scare to the new infidel of civil liberties, Attorney General John Ashcroft and the Patriot Act; and from colonial outposts in Cuba and the Philippines to the postcolonial occupations of Iraq and Puerto Rico—the need for a public moral voice and schooling for social justice has never been more urgent or seldom less apparent.

Historically, assaults on the public trust and incursions into democratic liberties have been met by—among others—public intellectuals who recognized the moral dimension of education and the social responsibility of educators. Some also embraced this moral charge during the renaissance in curriculum studies, most notably Dwayne Huebner (1975a, 1975b), James Macdonald (1975), Alex Molnar (1987), and David Purpel (1989). Today, curriculum workers must advocate *within* the public square for a moral education in which curriculum and pedagogy for human dignity, social and economic justice, spiritual enlightenment, and peace and sustainability are the new standards of excellence.

The Millennial Generation of Curriculum Workers

Banishing curriculum traditionalists from the cathedrals of curriculum thought, we created "complicated conversations" as well as rifts of complicated relationships (Pinar et al. 1995). This post-Tylerian transformation soon morphed into a postmodern pastiche of intellectual discourses that has come to characterize the field at the beginning of the new millennium. Employing critical social theory, feminist thought, psychoanalysis, critical postmodernism, queer theory, phenomenology, and eschatology—to name but a few of the multitude of contemporary curriculum genres—this group of cacophonous voices has begotten a millennial generation of curricularists who do not work on the margins of curriculum studies (Sears 2003).

Reengaging with practitioners who chose to work along the margins of curriculum practice is the next critical turning point for our field. It is difficult work, and, as pointed out in the first anthology of selected papers from the inaugural Curriculum and Pedagogy conference, it is work that

> must be done in the context of a supportive disciplinary community, and public intellectual activities must be designed and enacted in specific educational settings. Theory must be generated and then turned into practice: a *disciplinary* professionalism must result in the enactment of a civic professionalism. This "double" professionalism will not be easy, given the current separation of theory and practice in the curriculum field. (Henderson and Kesson 2001, 3)

As disciplinary and civic professionals, curriculum workers *engage* with others. Former "practitioners"—committed to education as a public moral enterprise—develop, implement, and modify curriculum in collaboration with "theorists" who dedicate themselves to generating grounded theory through such educational engagement. Committed to crossing the borderland between theory and practice, both believe that the synergistic reciprocity between ideas (which inform action) and experience (which generates concepts) brings a renewed commitment to the public moral enterprise that is the soul of curriculum work.

Scholar–practitioners have taken up this challenge of praxis. Marilyn Doerr (2000, 2004) has adapted *currere* (Pinar 1974a) in teaching high school ecology through "environmental autobiography," while others (such as Marsh et al. 1990; McCutcheon 1995; Wood 1990) have sought to reconceptualize school curriculum development through collaborative deliberation. Jim Henderson's work on transformative curriculum (Henderson and Hawthorne 2000; Henderson and Kesson 2003), inspired by Dewey, grounded on the work of Schwab (1978), and rooted in the work of his mentor, Eisner, has reengaged school administrators. Susan Finley (2001) has appropriated a curriculum of caring to her work with students and teacher educators and their work with homeless youth and their families. Michael Apple and Jim Beane (1995; Beane 1997) have developed a curriculum integration process for democratic education centered on students with the work of classroom teachers (such as Brodhagen, 1995; Brodhagen, Weilbacher, and Beane 1998).

Arguing for the need of middle-level philosophy—similar to Klohr's usage of middle-range theorizing a generation earlier (Brooks 2001)—and building on the work of Greene (1988), Joanne Arhar, a college professor, and Rebecca McElfresh, a school principal, detail in this book how interdisciplinarity can be a "site of transformation rather than resolution" and also a form of action research (see also Arhar, Holly, and Kasten 2000). Similarly, Gaztambide-Fernández (2002)—an artist schooled in classical music turned educator grounded in critical pedagogy—has engaged in midrange theorizing to challenge Eisner's conception of the arts as a *model* for education and to suggest how it is a *modality* for educating in the possibilities of the "now."

Educating *through* the arts is precisely the approach advanced by Tom Poetter (2002) through his collaborative fictional writing project among practitioners and academics on the impact of high stakes testing. He observes,

> [W]e no doubt like to think that when our students or constituents read our work it has an impact on the theorizing and practice they do in curriculum and pedagogy. But the fact of the matter is that few people are reading our work. . . . [F]iction is one powerful way to reach people. (4–5)

Out of that project, a junior high school teacher and two local education professors penned one of the most engaging stories. "The Illusion of Inclusion" is a tale of several innovative and soon-to-be "subordinate" educators at Windwood Junior High School who struggle against the district's decision to impose a "one-dimensional, 'canned' curriculum" in order to improve aggregate test scores (Weilbacher, Ochs, and Ehlers-Zavala 2002, 21).

In addition to employing different modalities, the new curriculum worker must relearn to "teach again and again" (Brice, Eggebeen, and Reid 2003). For example, when a first-grade teacher, a middle school science teacher, and a university social studies professor engaged in dialogue about teaching for democracy, they used narrative and life history methods. Following their narratives, they conclude,

> While we were certain we believed in equitable and empowering learning, we came to recognize a potent difference between our rhetoric about such learning and its manifestation in our teaching. . . . As educators, we are all pressed with mandates that direct us toward more and more standardization and conventional teaching practices. Having interrogated our beliefs and practices, we found we could not return to a conventional, inherited curriculum. (169–70)

These educators rightly caution that "sustaining our revitalized commitments is not easy" (170). Further, not all such collaborative experiences are transformative—at least in the manner anticipated. Integrating (and reconceptualizing) cutting-edge curriculum theory into everyday educational practice is—to use an inelegant phrase—a messy process. This is detailed no better than in the struggles chronicled in this book by Morna McDermott, Toby Daspit, and Kevin Dodd as they applied the work of Freire (1970) and Boal (1985) to a weeklong experience with school district participants. Their expectation of simply offering "drama and social transformation in three easy steps—just add water" (73) met headlong with the realities of en masse desertion by workshop participants.

Despite its messiness, its uncertainty, and its difficulty, there is a moral imperative to pursue curriculum praxis. The postmillennial curriculum worker is engaged: developing curriculum materials for peace education, interrogating issues of race and racism in the Euro-centered classroom, exploring with students the seamy underbelly of the global economy, challenging heteronormativity and the consequent heterosexism and homophobia, and so forth. In these engagements, ours is an intellectual role as we immerse ourselves in public work—in this case, schools. To do otherwise perpetuates atheoretical practice and promulgates ungrounded theory. In the process of doing this work, we produce curriculum scholarship that, as Goodman (2003) asserts, "helps its audience to gain insight into some aspect of the human condition (e.g., education) in ways that are personally and socially meaningful" (xvii). He goes on,

> We would be wise to remember Dewey's contention that scholarship is most useful when it begins and ends, that is, when it is thoroughly grounded in human experience. . . . Dewey believed that the most important and perhaps unique role of the intellectual in our imperfect democracy is to help our community avoid cultural stagnation as well as violent revolutions by fostering and supporting meaningful, substantive, and authentic reform. (xviii)

Toward this end, curriculum workers are public moral intellectuals who work within an embryonic democracy unafraid of stirring controversy, stimulating critical analysis, challenging orthodoxy, pursuing collaboration, and searching for consensus. Toward that end, curriculum workers—ranging from elementary science teachers and school district curriculum coordinators to professors of curriculum and textbook authors—must share in this ongoing curriculum conversation that began a century ago. That is our calling as progressive educators committed to collaborative curriculum development.

References

Alberty, H. 1947. *Reorganizing the high school curriculum.* New York: Macmillan.

Apple, M. 1979. *Ideology and curriculum.* New York: Routledge & Kegan Paul.

Apple, M., and J. Beane, eds. 1995. *Democratic schools.* Alexandria, Va.: Association for Supervision and Curriculum Development.

Arhar, J. M., M. L. Holly, and W. Kasten. 2000. *Action research for teachers: Traveling the yellow brick road.* Columbus: Merrill/Prentice Hall.

Beane, J. 1997. *Curriculum integration: Designing a core of democratic education.* New York: Teachers College Press.

Bestor, A. 1953. *Educational wastelands.* Urbana: University of Illinois Press.

Boal, A. 1985. *Theatre of the oppressed.* Translated by C. McBride and M. McBride. New York: Theatre Communications Group.

Bond, H. 1934. *The education of the Negro in the American social order.* New York: Prentice Hall.

———. 1939. *Negro education in America.* Washington, D.C.: Associated Publishers.

Brameld, T. 1965. *Education as power.* New York: Holt, Rinehart and Winston.

Brice, L., E. Eggebeen, and J. Reid. 2003. Learning to teach again and again. In *Curriculum and pedagogy for peace and sustainability,* edited by L. Anderson Allen et al. Troy, N.Y.: Educators International Press, 157–70.

Brodhagen, B. 1995. The situation made us special. In *Democratic schools,* edited by M. Apple and J. Beane. Alexandria, Va.: Association for Supervision and Curriculum Development, 83–100.

Brodhagen, B., G. Weilbacher, and J. Beane. 1998. What we've learned from "living in the future." In *The curriculum: Problems, politics, and possibilities,* 2nd ed., edited by M. Apple and L. Beyer. Albany: State University of New York Press, 117–33.

Brooks, N. 2001. Paul Klohr and the second wave. In *Democratic curriculum theory and practice: Retrieving public spaces,* edited by K. Sloan and J. Sears. New York: Educators International Press, 49–65.

Caswell, H., and D. Campbell. 1935. *Curriculum development.* New York: American Book Company.

Clandinin, J., and M. Connelly. 1987. Teachers' personal practical knowledge. *Journal of Curriculum Studies* 19(6): 487–500.

———. 1988. Study teachers' knowledge of classrooms. *Journal of Educational Thought* 22(2): 269–82.

———. 1992. Teacher as curriculum maker. In *Handbook of research on curriculum,* edited by P. Jackson. New York: Macmillan, 363–401.

Corey, S. 1953. *Action research to improve school practices.* New York: Teachers College, Columbia University.

Cremin, L. 1961. *The transformation of the school: Progressivism in American education, 1876–1957.* New York: Vintage.

Doerr, M. 2000. A high school ecology curriculum employing *currere:* A critical postmodern approach to pedagogy. Doctoral diss., Pennsylvania State University.

———. 2004. *Currere and the environmental autobiography: A phenomenological approach to the teaching of ecology.* New York: Peter Lang.

Duckworth, E. 1986. Teaching as research. *Harvard Educational Review* 56(4): 481–95.

———. 1987. *The having of wonderful ideas and other essays.* New York: Teachers College Press.

Eisner, E. 1979. *The educational imagination: On the design and evaluation of school programs.* New York: Macmillan.

Ellsworth, E. 1989. Why doesn't this feel empowering? Working through the repressive myths of critical pedagogy. *Harvard Educational Review* 59(3): 297–324.

Finley, S. 2001. From the streets to the classrooms: Street intellectuals as teacher educators, collaborations in revolutionary pedagogy. In *Democratic curriculum theory and practice: Retrieving public spaces*, edited by K. Sloan and J. Sears. New York: Educators International Press, 113–26.

Flesch, R. 1955. *Why Johnny can't read*. New York: Harper.

Freire, P. 1970. *Pedagogy of the oppressed*. New York: Herder & Herder.

Gaztambide-Fernández, R. 2002. (De)constructing art as a model/(re)constructing art as a possibility: An interactive essay exploring the possibilities of the arts in relationship to education. In *In(Ex)clusion: (Re)visioning the democratic ideal*, edited by T. Poetter, C. Haerr, M. Hayes, C. Higgins, and K. Baptist. Troy, N.Y.: Educators International Press, 83–107.

Goodman, J. 2003. Foreword: Some reflections on the purpose of curriculum scholarship. In *Curriculum and pedagogy for peace and sustainability*, edited by L. Anderson Allen et al. Troy, N.Y.: Educators International Press, xiii–xx.

Goodson, I. 1992. Sponsoring the teachers' voice: Teachers' lives and teacher development. *Understanding teacher development*, edited by A. Hargreaves and M. Fullan. New York: Teachers College Press, 110–21.

Greene, M. 1978. *Landscapes of learning*. New York: Teachers College Press.

———. 1988. *The dialectic of freedom*. New York: Teachers College Press.

Henderson, J., and R. Hawthorne. 2000. *Transformative curriculum leadership*. 2nd ed. Upper Saddle River, N.J.: Merrill/Prentice Hall.

Henderson, J., and K. Kesson. 2001. Curriculum work as public intellectual leadership. In *Democratic curriculum theory and practice: Retrieving public spaces*, edited by K. Sloan and J. Sears. New York: Educators International Press, 1–23.

———. 2003. *Curriculum wisdom: Educational decisions in democratic societies*. Upper Saddle River, N.J.: Pearson Merrill Prentice Hall.

Huebner, D. 1975a. Poetry and power: The politics of curriculum development. In *Curriculum theorizing: The reconceptualists*, edited by W. Pinar. Berkeley, Calif.: McCutchan, 271–80.

———. 1975b. The tasks of the curricular theorist. In *Curriculum theorizing: The reconceptualists*, edited by W. Pinar. Berkeley, Calif.: McCutchan, 250–70.

Jackson, P. 1979. Curriculum and its discontents. *Curriculum Inquiry* 10(1): 28–43.

Kliebard, H. 1967. Special issue on curriculum. *Theory into Practice* 6(4).

———. 1986. *The struggle for the American curriculum, 1893–1958*. Boston: Routledge & Kegan Paul.

Klohr, P. 1967. This issue. *Theory into Practice* 6(4); 165.

Lobdell, P. 1984. The Marietta Johnson school of organic education. Doctoral diss., Auburn University.

Macdonald, J. 1975. Curriculum theory. In *Curriculum theorizing: The reconceptualists*, edited by W. Pinar. Berkeley, Calif.: McCutchan, 5–13.

Mager, R. 1962. *Preparing instructional objectives*. Palo Alto, Calif.: Fearon.

Marsh, C., C. Day, L. Hannay, and G. McCutcheon. 1990. *Reconceptualizing school-based curriculum development*. Bristol, Pa.: Falmer.

Marshall, J., J. Sears, and D. Adair. 2001. Small gatherings, shifting coalitions and communities of discourses. In *Democratic curriculum theory and practice: Retrieving public spaces*, edited by K. Sloan and J. Sears. New York: Educators International Press, 25–47.

Marshall, J., J. Sears, and W. Schubert. 2000. *Turning points in curriculum*. Upper Saddle River, N.J.: Prentice Hall.

McCutcheon, G. 1995. *Developing the curriculum: Solo and group deliberation*. New York: Longman.

McNally, H., and A. Passow. 1960. *Improving the quality of public school programs: Approaches to curriculum development*. New York: Teachers College, Columbia University.

Miel, A. 1946. *Changing the curriculum: A social process*. New York: Appleton-Century.

Miller, J. 1990a. *Creating spaces and finding voices: Teachers collaborating for empowerment*. Albany: State University of New York Press.

———. 1990b. Teachers as curriculum makers. In *Teaching and thinking about curriculum*, edited by J. Sears and D. Marshall. New York: Teachers College Press, 85–96.

Molnar, A., ed. 1987. *Social issues and education*. Alexandria, Va.: Association for Supervision and Curriculum Development.

Parker, F. 1894. *Talks on pedagogics*. New York: Kellog.

Pinar, W. 1974a. *Currere*: Toward reconceptualization. In *Basic problems in modern education*, edited by J. Jelinek. Tempe: Arizona State University, College of Education, 144–71. Reprinted in W. Pinar, ed. (1975), *Curriculum theorizing: The reconceptualists*. Berkeley, Calif.: McCutchan, 396–414.

———. 1988. Introduction. In *Contemporary curriculum discourses*, edited by W. Pinar. Scottsdale, Ariz.: Gorsuch Scarisbrick, 1–13.

———. 1992. "Dreamt into existence by others": Curriculum theory and school reform. *Theory into Practice* 31(3): 228–35.

———, ed. 1974b. *Heightened consciousness, cultural revolution and curriculum theory*. Berkeley, Calif.: McCutchan.

———, ed. 1975. *Curriculum theorizing: The reconceptualists*. Berkeley, Calif.: McCutchan.

Pinar, W., and M. Grumet. 1976. *Toward a poor curriculum*. Dubuque, Iowa: Kendall/Hunt.

Pinar, W., W. Reynolds, P. Slattery, and P. Taubman. 1995. *Understanding curriculum: An introduction to the study of historical and contemporary curriculum discourses*. New York: Peter Lang.

Poetter, T. 2002. Opening myself up to writing fiction. In *In(Ex)clusion: (Re)visioning the democratic ideal*, edited by T. Poetter, C. Haerr, M. Hayes, C. Higgins, and K. Baptist. Troy, N.Y.: Educators International Press, 1–12.

Purpel, D. 1989. *The moral and spiritual crisis in education: A curriculum for justice and compassion in education*. South Hadley, Mass.: Bergin & Garvey.

Rugg, H. 1938. *Man and his changing world*. New York: Teachers College, Columbia University.

Saylor, J. G. 1941. *Factors associated with participation in cooperative programs of curriculum development*. New York: Teachers College, Columbia University.

Schubert, W. 1986. *Curriculum: Perspective, paradigm, and possibility*. New York: Macmillan.

———. 1989. Teacher lore: A neglected basis for understanding curriculum and supervision. *Journal of Curriculum and Supervision* 4(2): 282–85.

———. 1991. Teacher lore: A basis for understanding praxis. In *Stories lives tell: Narrative and dialogue in education*, edited by C. Witherell and N. Noddings. New York: Teachers College Press, 207–33.

Schubert, W., and W. Ayers. 1992. *Teacher lore: Learning from our own experience*. New York: Longman.

Schubert, W., and A. Lopez-Schubert, eds. 1982. *Conceptions of curriculum knowledge: Focus on students and teachers*. State College: College of Education, Penn State University.

Schubert, W., A. Lopez-Schubert, T. Thomas, and W. Carroll. 2002. *Curriculum books: The first hundred years*. 2nd ed. New York: Peter Lang.

Schwab, J. 1969. The practical: A language for curriculum. *School Review* 78(1): 1–23.

———. 1978. *Science, curriculum, and liberal education: Selected essays*. Chicago: University of Chicago Press.

Sears, J. 1985. Rethinking teacher education. *Journal of Curriculum Theorizing* 6(3): 24–79.

———. 1992. The second wave of curriculum theorizing: Labyrinths, orthodoxies, and other legacies of the glass bead game. *Theory into Practice* 31(3): 210–18.

———. 2003. From margin to center: On the "other" side of the curriculum renaissance. *Curriculum Inquiry* 33(4): 427–39.

Sears, J., and J. Marshall. 2000. Generational influences on contemporary curriculum thought. *Journal of Curriculum Studies* 32(2): 199–214.

Smith, E., and R. Tyler. 1942. *Appraising and recording student progress*. New York: Harper.

Stratemeyer, F. 1931. *The effective use of curriculum materials*. New York: Teachers College, Columbia University.

Stratemeyer, F., H. Forkner, and M. McKim. 1947. *Developing a curriculum for modern living*. New York: Teachers College, Columbia University.

Taba, H. 1950. *Elementary curriculum in intergroup relations*. Washington, D.C.: American Council on Education.

———. 1962. *Curriculum development*. New York: Harcourt, Brace and World.

Tanner, D., and L. Tanner. 1995. *Curriculum development*. 3rd ed. Columbus: Merrill.

Tyler, R. 1949. *Basic principles of curriculum and instruction*. Chicago: University of Chicago Press.

Urban, W. 1992. *Black scholar: Horace Mann Bond, 1904–1972*. Athens: University of Georgia Press.

Weilbacher, G., K. Ochs, and F. Ehlers-Zavala. 2002. The illusion of inclusion. In *In(Ex)clusion: (Re)visioning the democratic ideal*, edited by T. Poetter, C. Haerr, M. Hayes, C. Higgins, and K. Baptist. Troy, N.Y.: Educators International Press, 13–39.

Wood, G. 1990. Teachers as curriculum workers. In *Teaching and thinking about curriculum*, edited by J. Sears and D. Marshall. New York: Teachers College Press, 97–109.

Zirbes, L. 1935. *Curriculum trends*. Washington, D.C.: Association for Childhood Education.

Blurring the Borderlands: Imagining New Relationships

2

JOANNE M. ARHAR, KENT STATE UNIVERSITY
REBECCA McELFRESH, HUDSON CITY SCHOOLS, HUDSON, OHIO

The Opportunity of Our Crisis

We live in challenging times. On the one hand, we are exploring new ways of engaging our work together as K–12 and university-based educators, searching for human wholeness, justice, and the sustainability of our planet. The voices of those who struggle to close the opportunity gap, which is deeply embedded within the social and cultural inequalities of our society and are promoted by our educational system, inform our work. We embrace a particular, holistic view of teaching and learning with the potential to form a praxis that blurs the boundaries of theory and practice. On the other hand, a political agenda designed to serve its own goals—accountability through standardized testing and choice—aligns the purposes of teacher education and K–12 schools in ways that run counter to the previously described vision. Theory and practice are thus connected by educational policies as stated in the federal legislation of 2001, the No Child Left Behind Act (U.S. Department of Education 2001), and further bolstered by the secretary of education's Annual Report on Teacher Quality (U.S. Department of Education 2002a).

Teacher preparation programs and schools have come a long way in their work together. University professors teach classes in schools, and school-based faculty and administrators teach classes in universities. Teacher educators consider themselves practitioners as well as theorists and researchers, and school-based teachers are involved in rigorous action inquiry projects with colleagues in K–12 schools and universities. Extensive field experiences have become the sine qua non of many teacher preparation programs. Through these field experiences, we hope to build and sustain relationships that transform teaching and learning around the problems of practice.

Yet the theory/practice gap remains evident in the daily work of school and university-based faculties. Teacher education programs typically embody progressive principles, while schools, responding to the mandates of the state, are more likely to use traditional teaching methods. Research is still "conducted on" and the results "delivered to" schools by university researchers, while schools continue to search for research-based answers to burning questions of practice. Discussions about teacher preparation programs occur apart from K–12 faculties, but universities wish placement for their students, and public schools seek consultation services for professional development. Reward structures make fluidity between university and K–12 educators difficult at best, with significant implications for career development and financial well-being. For instance, teachers cannot afford the pay cuts inherent in a move to the university, and university faculty who are deeply involved in the daily life of schools take longer to publish and sometimes risk tenure and promotion. Schools blame teacher education programs for not adequately preparing teachers for the exigencies of urban education, but rarely have we joined together to imagine new ways to work together in a professional learning community.

Differing Ideologies

The opposing views articulated here frame our discussion of differing ideologies of teaching and learning, teacher quality, and teacher education. We draw on the one hand from educational policy as articulated by the federal government and on the other from middle-level professional educational organizations whose approach embodies progressive ideals. Two documents will serve as a point of discussion on federal educational policy: the No Child Left Behind Act (NCLB) of 2001 and the secretary of education's Annual Report on Teacher Quality (U.S. Department of Education 2002a). The perspective of middle-level education will be drawn from policy statements from the National Middle School Association (2002a, 2002b) and the National Forum to Accelerate Middle Grades Reform (2002). Through a discussion of these two perspectives, we will argue for a new vision of partnerships between university-based educators and K–12 public educators.

Vision of Education

The National Forum to Accelerate Middle Grades Reform (2002) offers a vision of middle-level education that involves academic excellence, developmental responsiveness, and social equity:

1. [Academically excellent schools] "challenge all students to use their minds well, providing them with the curriculum, instruction, assessment, support, and time they need to meet rigorous academic standards. . . . The curriculum and extra curricular programs in such schools are challenging and engaging, tapping young adolescents' boundless energy, interests, and curiosity.

2. Developmentally responsive [schools] . . . create small learning communities of adults and students in which stable, close, and mutually respectful relationships support all students' intellectual, ethical, and social growth. . . . [They] involve families as partners in the education of their children. These schools are deeply rooted in their communities.

3. Socially equitable schools . . . seek to keep their students' future options open. They have high expectations for all their students and are committed to helping each child produce work of high quality. These schools make sure that all students are in academically rigorous classes, staffed by experienced and expertly prepared teachers. These teachers acknowledge and honor their students' histories and cultures. They work to educate every child well and to overcome systematic variation in resources and outcomes related to race, class, gender and ability.

The NCLB advocates as its vision of education four major points aimed to reduce the achievement gap between students from different groups and in essence provide more equitable education for all students. First, more accountability for results is to be accomplished by frequent standardized testing with results reported for subgroups. Second, states will have more flexibility and freedom to direct their federal education funding. Third, federal dollars are targeted for scientifically tested programs. Fourth, parents with a child enrolled in a "failing" school will have greater choice in school selection.

Learning and Teaching

The National Research Council (2000) defines learning as a process of developing usable knowledge (not just isolated facts) building on previous knowledge and experience, understanding and organizing information in a conceptual framework, and monitoring progress toward learning goals. The secretary of education's Annual Report on Teacher Quality (U.S. Department of Education 2002a), on the other hand, defines learning as receiving information and demonstrating it on a standardized test.

Decades of research on teaching and teacher preparation (such as Richardson 2001; Wideen, Mayer-Smith, and Moon 1998; Wilson, Floden, and Ferrini-Mundy 2001; Wittrock 1986) define quality teaching as a complex process of

> [r]epresenting complex knowledge in accessible ways, asking good questions, forming relationships with students and parents, collaborating with other professionals, interpreting multiple data sources, meeting the needs of students with widely varying abilities and background, and both posing and solving problems of practice. (Cochran-Smith 2002, 380)

In contrast, the secretary of education defines a quality teacher as one "who has obtained full state certification as a teacher (including certification obtained through alternative routes) or passed the state teacher licensing examination, and holds a license to teach in such state" (U.S. Department of Education 2002a, 4). The secretary of education further emphasizes the importance of high verbal ability in the transmission of subject matter knowledge.

Teacher Education

A synthesis of research on teacher education prepared by Wilson et al. (2001) and funded by the U.S. Department of Education indicates that there is evidence that teacher education *does* contribute to teacher quality. According to this report, "[T]here is value-added by teacher preparation" (14), and "prospective teachers need to reorganize their subject matter knowledge into knowledge about how to teach subject matter to diverse students" (15). The National Middle School Association (2002b) also supports the need for strong teacher preparation:

> Quality teachers must have content knowledge and know how to teach that knowledge to young adolescents. Focusing exclusively or predominantly on content knowledge, at the expense of professional preparation "methods" training, will be less effective in the overall learning of middle level students.

The secretary of education's Annual Report on Teacher Quality comes to a different conclusion: "There is little scientific evidence that knowledge of pedagogy, degrees in education, amount of time spent practice teaching have any significant relationship to student achievement" (8).

How do we make sense of these disparate views underlying so many of the difficulties that schools and universities have in coming together? How can we approach them to transform what appears conflicting and dichotomous into some new whole? What does it require of university- and school-based educators to blur the borderlands that have tradition- ally separated us? What can we learn from each position that will benefit children as we prepare teachers to work with them? To explore these two approaches to education, we begin by looking at some foundational concepts.

Quality Research

While almost everyone agrees that we need more high-quality research to help schools improve, federal policy and professional educational organiza- tions differ on what constitutes quality research. The NCLB requires fed- eral grantees to use their funds on "scientifically based research" and for "explanation[s] of why the activities are expected to improve student aca- demic achievement." The law includes definitions of research quality that are further developed in the Department of Education's Strategic Plan for 2002–2007 (U.S. Department of Education 2002b). "Evidence-based practices" and "scientific based research," mentioned over one hundred times in the NCLB, have become code words for randomized experimental studies in which participants, programs, or activities are assigned to differ- ent "treatments" with appropriate "controls" so that an "effect" can be "measured." Methods must be presented with sufficient detail and clarity for replication so that a research base can be built on the findings of pre- vious studies. Strategic Goal 4, for instance, is to

> [t]ransform education into an evidence-based field. Unlike medicine, agri- culture, and industrial production, the field of education operates largely on the basis of ideology and professional consensus. As such, it is subject to fads and is incapable of the cumulative progress that follows from the application of the scientific methods and from the systematic collection and use of objective information in policy making. We will change educa- tion to make it an evidence-based field. (50)

While there is a great deal of controversy about whether educational research is better or worse than medical research and whether we should seek to emulate the methods of medical research, it is the definition of randomized research design that is the focus of our interest. Some educational researchers and theorists argue that science is more than a method or a search for certainty through causal analysis. David Berliner (2002), the former president of the American Educational Research Association and a researcher who engages in large-scale experimental studies, finds other definitions of science to be more appropriate to the work of educational researchers:

> I admire Richard Feynman's (1999) definition of science as "the belief in the ignorance of authority" (p. 187). Unrestricted questioning is what gives science its energy and vibrancy. Values, religion, politics, vested material interests, and the like can distort our scientific work only to the extent that they stifle challenges to authority, curtailing the questioning of whatever orthodoxy exits. Unfettered, science will free itself from false beliefs or, at the least, will moderate the climate in which those beliefs exist. (18)

Erickson and Gutierrez (2002) argue that there is a danger in the imposition of evidence-based social engineering approach to educational reform. The federal government should not be in the business of mandating a particular method of inquiry. Whereas an experimental study might ask, "Did it work?" a qualitative study might ask, "*How* did it work?" According to the authors, the value of qualitative research is that it suggests both how and why particular treatments work. This is important information in a field that is as complex as teaching, where replicability has always been problematic. "Educational treatments are situated and dynamically interactive. They are locally constructed social ways of life involving continual monitoring and mutual adjustment among persons, not relatively replicable entities like chemical compounds" (21).

The federal mandate also undermines the value of practitioner-based research, which is highly valued by some practitioner educational organizations. Every year the National Middle School Association features sessions on action research at its national conference and has recently announced an award for high-quality action research studies. Action research is distinguished from other forms of basic and applied research in that it is conducted by practitioners in their own context rather than by outsiders, emphasizes how things work in a specific setting, has an explicit value orientation (that is, it seeks to democratize teaching and schooling), and is geared toward the improvement of the practitioner–researcher as well as the practice (Arhar, Holly, and Kasten 2000). The power of action research lies in bridging theory, research, and practice as teachers enhance their professionalism in collegial groups.

Teaching and learning are complex processes that depend on the context in which they occur, making educational research complex and difficult. Anyone who has ever tried to replicate a program successful in one setting understands the problems associated with generalizability. While the quantitative methods advocated by the Department of Education's (2002b) Strategic Plan for 2002–2007 provide information about the impact of a given practice, they fail to provide the rich, contextual understanding made available through qualitative methods.

Contexts of the Dissonance

Differing Notions of Democracy

Bruce Novak (2002) describes two historic understandings of democracy that inform our discussion of these views of educational reform. He traces the intellectual legacy of libertarian forms of democracy through the work of Alexis de Tocqueville and John Stuart Mill. In reaction to libertarian forms of democracy, he describes the communitarian notion of democracy, based on a collective and humanized search for the greater good, through the work of Matthew Arnold. We find evidence of both in our current political milieu.

Tocqueville's (1833) notion of democracy evolved from his deep concern that the United States would become ruled by a tyranny of the majority. He argued strongly that exercising individual rights and responsibilities would avoid control from an uninvolved majority. These libertarian roots inform the philosophy of the Republican Party and the politics of the Right. Mill's (1859) concept of individual liberty is grounded in part on Tocqueville's thinking on individual rights. Mill advocated for a laissez-faire government, one that should only help those unable to reason because of their age or their development. Disciplined reason was necessary for those unprepared for individual liberty. Mill's

libertarian ideals extended to education as he advocated for the legislation of educational standards as a means to develop the disciplined mind
capable of reasoning.

Rather than focusing on individual liberty as a means of sustaining democracy, Matthew Arnold (1901), a nineteenth-century Victorian thinker,
advocated for a democracy that focused on a *common* pursuit of happiness:

> The essential ingredients for such a democracy were more than political
> enfranchisement, more than free economic and cultural trade, more even
> than a system of public education. Arnold quickly came to see that what
> was truly fundamental in forming such a social body was having, at the
> central focus of a national system of education, the creation of humane
> social environments and humanizing courses of study. (Novak 2002, 612)

Building on Arnold's perspective, Novak views the NCLB as a legislative attempt to produce a tranquilized democracy, one that will consolidate and
systematize the mind of a nation often unable to find a way to unite itself
and long tending toward anarchy.

Differing Notions of Freedom

Maxine Greene (1988) proposes a "dialectic of freedom" as a way to understand and transform the tension between these two views of educational
reform. This tension cannot be resolved in victory of one over the other or
in some perfect synthesis but rather by recognizing the obstacles to freedom
and acting on them in some existential project. She argues that freedom has
taken a libertarian meaning of self-dependence and self-determination
rather than a communitarian one of connectedness and community.

What Greene (1988) calls a "negative freedom" is "the right not to be
interfered with or coerced or compelled to do what one does not choose to
do (16). She asks how "in this positivist, media-dominated, and self-
centered time . . . with so much acquiescence and so much thoughtlessness
around us, are we to open people to the power of possibility?" (55). According to Greene, freedom is about opening spaces where none seem to exist, seeing the obstacles that appear in the everyday landscape of schooling,
viewing the taken for granted from multiple perspectives, imagining new
possibilities, and taking action. This action involves taking risks and creating alternatives that include caring and community, authoring our own lives,
establishing a reality of our own, and taking responsibility for ourselves.

This does not happen, Greene asserts, when freedom is taken as an individual right accompanied by deregulation from the federal government. This libertarian notion of freedom underlies the principle of consumer choice and market rationality that supposedly will ensure that good schools will gain students and that bad schools will go away. The principle of choice may give false hope because it does nothing to challenge deeper social and cultural inequalities (Apple 2001). Whitty (1997) argues,

> Atomized decision-making in a highly stratified society may appear to give everyone equal opportunities, but transforming responsibility for decision-making from the public to the private sphere can actually reduce the scope for collective action to improve the quality of education for all. (41)

How are we to see beyond the taken-for-granted commonplaces so that we can name the obstacles to freedom? What does this require of us as teachers and as students?

Differing Notions of Reform

Schools serving poor children are in need of radical change. The achievement gap between white and black students is only one indicator of the problem. Children in schools that serve predominantly poor communities are not being provided the kind of education that will help them gain access to the social capital afforded to students in wealthy schools. Democrats and Republicans could not have agreed to the sweeping changes entailed in the NCLB if they did not agree, at least, on this.

However, standards-based, choice-based, and accountability-based proposals, as embodied in the NCLB, are inadequate to address inequities in schooling. But progressive critiques from the Left often lack concrete action steps that will benefit children in high-poverty schools. For example, forced busing for the purpose of desegregation failed to provide equal educational experiences for children in urban settings. Clearly, polarizing views of school reform are not serving students or educators well.

Blurring the Borderlands

Perhaps the crises in urban schools and the very different proposals for educational reform that we have outlined will spur us to think of new ways of being together. To distance ourselves from these polar views, we propose placing freedom for professional judgment and personal responsibility for the consequences in the hands of school- and university-based teachers working together.

Kegan (1994, 320) suggests that the postmodern view bids disputants to do several things: (1) consider that you and your opponent have identified the poles of the conflict, (2) realize that the conflict is an expression of the incompleteness of each taken as completeness, (3) value the relationship as an opportunity to live out your own multiplicity, and (4) focus on ways to allow the conflictual relationship to transform the parties rather than the parties resolving the conflict. As Kegan suggests, identifying the poles of the conflict, as we have done here, is the first step toward transforming our views of the dissonance. But what else can we do? Professional development schools and town hall meetings that bring together diverse stakeholders around issues of educational importance are two proposals for the mutual reform of schools and teacher preparation programs. But to many educators, association with their disciplines is most important. Recognizing the need to engage in transformative dialogue as proposed by Kegan, we propose a way to challenge the professional routines embedded within our structure of separate disciplines to imagine new spaces for action. This is where an interdisciplinary dialogue might prove instructive.

The Perspective of Interdisciplinary Dialogue

While the disciplines may not be sufficient in themselves to move beyond simple politics, they are a starting point for those of us embedded in their structures. They can provide a lens for seeing beyond the commonplaces of education in both schools and universities. What might each discipline offer to us? How can a dialogue among those with differing visions use interdisciplinarity as a site of transformation rather than resolution? Each discipline offers its own frame of reference, its own structure of knowledge that contributes to our understandings. Art, for instance, "is committed to that perception of the world which alienates individuals from their functional existence and performance in society" (Marcuse 1978, 9). Through the study of history, sociology, politics, and anthropology, we can engage in critical reflection of the historical, social, economic, political, and cultural realities that shape our lives (Leistyna, Woodrum, and Sherblom 1996). The study of science, philosophy, and mathematics helps us understand the universe and humanity's relationship to nature in holistic ways. By constantly challenging our tacit assumptions about the infrastructure of concepts and ideas as new knowledge develops, we may avoid the fragmentation that occurs without such constant attention to change (Bohm and Peat 1987).

Moving beyond the talk of educational reform to what matters most to teachers (that is, the disciplines) may help problematize and deconstruct current practice, illuminating the ways in which our current configurations inhibit new vision. What are the cultural, political, and historical forces that frame and constrain our thinking? How are the prophetic voices of visual artists, poets, songwriters, and playwrights moving us to think differently about our views? What are the dissonances in our views? What part of a whole does my view represent? What in the view that you hold adds a richness and completeness to my view? What action project can we engage in that will allow us to inquire into our practice and that will allow us to grow professionally toward a higher order of consciousness?

These questions set the stage for an action project as proposed by Arhar et al. (2000) in which collaborative groups seek to address questions related to mutual research interests. An action agenda would address important questions of research design, such as, What will we try in order to improve our practice? How will we document the process? How will we verify that our judgments are trustworthy, credible, and respectful? How will we interpret the data? How will we portray what we have learned and make it public? How will these actions make life better? What will we do next?

We remain reflective as we approach this work, taking into consideration the larger goals of our work and its importance for the full realization of democratic living within our universities and schools. This is difficult work and requires our best energies as we envision new possibilities. Greene (1995) writes,

> More and more of us, for all our postmodern preoccupations, are aware of how necessary it is to keep such visions of possibilities before our eyes in the face of rampant carelessness, alienation and fragmentation. It is out of this kind of thinking, I still believe, that the ground of a critical community can be opened in our thinking and in our schools. (197–98)

References

Apple, M. 2001. *Educating the "right" way.* New York: Routledge.

Arhar, J. M., M. L. Holly, and W. Kasten. 2000. *Action research for teachers: Traveling the yellow brick road.* Columbus: Merrill/Prentice Hall.

Arnold, M. 1901. *Culture and anarchy: An essay in political criticism*. London: Smith and Elder.

Berliner, D. C. 2002. Educational research: The hardest science of all. *Educational Researcher* 31(8): 18–21.

Bohm, D., and F. D. Peat. 1987. *Science, order, and creativity: A dramatic new look at the creative roots of science and life*. New York: Bantam.

Cochran-Smith, M. 2002. Reporting on teacher quality: The politics of politics. *Journal of Teacher Education* 53(5): 379–82.

Erickson, F., and K. Gutierrez. 2002. Culture, rigor, and science in educational research. *Educational Researcher* 31(8): 21–24.

Greene, M. 1988. *The dialectic of freedom*. New York: Teachers College Press.

———. 1995. *Releasing the imagination*. San Francisco: Jossey-Bass.

Kegan, R. 1994. *In over our heads: The mental demands of modern life*. Cambridge, Mass.: Harvard University Press.

Leistyna, P., A. Woodrum, and S. A. Sherblom, eds. 1996. *Breaking free: The transformative power of critical pedagogy*. Cambridge, Mass.: Harvard Educational Review.

Marcuse, H. 1978. *The aesthetic dimension*. Boston: Beacon Press.

Mill, J. S. 1859. *On liberty*. London: J. W. Parker.

National Forum to Accelerate Middle Grades Reform. 2002. *Vision statement*. www.mgforum.org.vision.asp (accessed December 12, 2001).

National Middle School Association. 2002a. NMSA/NCATE standards on middle level teacher preparation. http://nmsa.org (accessed December 12, 2002).

———. 2002b. Teacher preparation must include content and professional preparation. http://nmsa.org (accessed December 12, 2002).

National Research Council. 2000. *How people learn: Brain, mind, experience, and school*. Washington, D.C.: National Academy Press.

Novak, B. 2002. Humanizing democracy: Matthew Arnold's nineteenth-century call for a common, higher, educative pursuit of happiness and its relevance to twenty-first century democratic life. *American Educational Research Journal* 39(3): 593–637.

Richardson, V., ed. 2001. *Handbook of research on teaching*. 4th ed. Washington, D.C.: American Educational Research Association.

Tocqueville, A. de. 1835. *Democracy in America*. London: Saunders and Otley.

U.S. Department of Education. 2001. *No Child Left Behind Act of 2001: Reauthorization of the Elementary and Secondary Education Act*. www.nochildleftbehind.gov/next/overview.index.html (accessed June 13, 2003).

———. 2002a. *Meeting the highly qualified teachers challenge: The secretary's annual report on teacher quality*. Washington, D.C.: U.S. Department of Education, Office of Postsecondary Education.

———. 2002b. Strategic Plan for 2002–2007. www.ed.gov/pubs/ stratplan2002-07/index.html (accessed June 6, 2003).

Whitty, G. 1997. Creating quasi-markets in education. In *Review of research in education*, vol. 22, edited by M. W. Apple. Washington, D.C.: American Educational Research Association, 3–47.

Wideen, M., J. Mayer-Smith, and B. Moon. 1998. A critical analysis of research on learning to teach: Making the case for an ecological perspective on inquiry. *Review of Educational Research* 68(2): 130–78.

Wilson, S., R. Floden, and J. Ferrini-Mundy. 2001. *Teacher preparation research: Current knowledge, gaps, and recommendations*. Report prepared for the U.S. Department of Education. Seattle: University of Washington, Center on the Study of Teaching and Policy.

Wittrock, M. C., ed. 1986. *Handbook of research on teaching*. 3rd ed. New York: Macmillan.

"Show Me the Money": Collaboration and a New Politics of School Knowledge

BARBARA BRODHAGEN, SHERMAN MIDDLE SCHOOL,
MADISON, WISCONSIN
MICHAEL W. APPLE, UNIVERSITY OF WISCONSIN, MADISON

Over the past three decades, critical educational studies have made major contributions to help educators understand the complex relationships between education and differential power. The dynamics of class, race, gender, and sexuality and how these are represented and struggled over in schools have been interrogated in powerful ways. Yet for all the gains, too often these interrogations have come from the balcony and are not sufficiently linked to the concrete realities of teachers' and students' lives or even to the very personal pedagogic and political agendas of teachers who attempt to build a practice based on critical perspectives (Apple 2001).

This chapter provides one "simple" example in which critical academics take leadership from critical practitioners and assist them in building a socially critical curriculum. This is the story of a group of middle school students and a widely known, critically oriented teacher—Barbara—engaging a former teachers' union president, critical academic, and activist—Michael—and his graduate students in answering questions about the economy, inequality, and their place in the world. This story has particular resonance today in a time when conservative forces have put immense pressure on educators to make closer connections both to an increasingly unequal labor market and to a curriculum based on dominant forms of knowledge (Apple 2001, 2003). Without a sense for the real possibility of interrupting these conservative forces, educators can either become cynical or have nowhere to turn for alternative and oppositional practices of teaching and curricula that actually work.

This is the story as seen through the eyes of Barbara and a racially and economically diverse group of middle school students.

Power and the Economy in the Seventh Grade

The seventh graders anxiously awaited their guests. A university professor and more than fifteen graduate students representing ten countries were coming to their classroom to interact with the students about their studies within the theme "Show Me the Money." It was not unusual for guests to visit their classroom. In fact, students had seen so many previous visitors that they thought they were supposed to be there as part of the team. But on this particular day, the seventh-grade students would be interviewing their international guests about their home country's economic systems, about young adolescents' place within their countries, and about what they and their fellow citizens thought the "American Dream" meant. How did this group of seventh-grade students get to this place?

Setting the Curricular Context

Approximately fifty students with diverse backgrounds, including some identified as having learning or emotional disabilities, and two full-time teachers had been working to create a collaborative democratic learning community in their classroom. Using curriculum integration as the organizing model, the group of students and teachers developed a list of themes to be studied over the course of one academic year. Through this approach, one represented, for example, in the widely used book *Democratic Schools* (Apple and Beane 1995), students participate in a curriculum planning process where they first generate questions about the Self and the World. In small groups and then with the whole class, students identify common questions and concerns and suggest names of themes when an idea or phrase captures the essence of overlapping questions from the Self and World lists (Beane 1993; Brodhagen 1995). Teachers are not passive in this process. They actively help students identify compelling themes that have intellectual, personal, and social importance. One of the themes suggested was "Show Me the Money."

In this unit there were four major concepts: History of Money (in the world and in the United States), Global Economy, Distribution of Wealth, and Personal Money Management. As part of the curriculum planning process, students suggest activities that might help them find answers to their questions. They suggest outside resources, such as individuals and possible material that could help build background knowledge or offer personal experience to bring meaning to a question or an issue. One of the ideas that the students had was to "talk to people from other countries about their money systems." Since both the classroom teachers involved were also graduate students working with Michael, they made arrangements to make this happen. They invited Michael to come in and to bring his current graduate students, who came from all over the world.

The middle school students engaged in a number of activities in preparation for their time with the international students. The students kept a "spending diary" for one week in which they recorded what they spent on nonessential items. They researched which countries were richest and how money systems in other countries were different from or the same as in the United States. This led to an important question: which countries would they research? The teachers suggested that students should go home and identify ten favorite pieces of clothing or possessions and find out where each had been made. Given the relations that the corporate sector in the United States had with poorly paid workers in Third World nations, this seemed like a wise suggestion. A list of the most frequently named countries was created, and pairs of students researched specific countries. They searched for detailed information, including the country's major exports and imports, the average per capita income, literacy rate, life expectancy, gross national product, and whether child labor was used, among other things. The class made a giant chart to record a portion of their research, including literacy and life expectancies and average per capita income.

With this preparation complete, Barbara and her coteacher invited Michael to come to class and tell the story of "cheap french fries" and to spend time answering questions about the issues the story raised. The story describes the connections between the mass consumption of cheap french fries in the United States and elsewhere and the exploitative labor, housing, health, and educational conditions in a Third World nation that grows the potatoes for the french fries sold by a well-known international chain of fast-food restaurants (Apple 1996). Michael did not hesitate to accept the invitation since he already knew a great deal about the theme and the purposes of the theme from earlier discussions with the teachers and had stressed to all his own undergraduate and graduate students the crucial importance of understanding, in an unreductive way (Apple 1995), the realities of the economy and its differential effects. Barbara's students had many questions for Michael, and many refused to believe that the french fries they consumed came from another country, let alone were acquired in the manner he described. Michael told the students that one of his students grew up in that country and that Michael himself had witnessed these conditions. When the students realized that this was not a "made-up" story, they were committed to finding out everything they could about how money works in the real economy.

Students returned to school with their completed spending diaries. They determined the range of spending and the average yearly expenditures of discretionary funds. They entered the amounts on the board and engaged in discussion. Most students were surprised; some were embarrassed to learn that they had more money to spend on nonessential items than many people earn in an entire year. Part of their discussion focused on why the United States has such a higher per capita income, how our natural resources are used, important economic laws, and why products often cost more if made in the United States.

The students then wanted to talk to people from other countries about their economic systems. Barbara and her coteacher invited an international group of their fellow graduate students to come. The seventh-grade students listed questions to interview their guests. These included the following:

1. When you first came to Madison, what was the biggest difference that you noticed? Was it what you expected?
2. How long have you been in school, and when you finish, what kind of job will you have? What is the average income for the job in your country, and how does it compare to the same job in the United States?
3. What role do children play in your economy?
4. What do people in your country think is the "American Dream"?
5. Michael Apple told us the story about "cheap french fries." Has there been a situation like this in your own country that involved the United States?

Small groups of students met with each of the graduate students and together conducted the interview. They recorded the answers, and when all the groups had finished, the entire class of seventh graders and the inter-national students came together for a general question-and-answer session and a debriefing. Barbara and Michael then had several discussions about the visit, about students' reactions, about the depth of their concerns, and about teachers' follow-up discussions. It was clear that students had pur-sued significant questions in meaningful ways. The conversation with Michael, the interviews with the international graduate students, and the process that ensued were important for the seventh graders. However, we must also note the lasting effects these experiences had on Michael and his students. While they have developed important skills to identify relations of dominance and subordination in schools, these critical researchers ben-efited from engaging issues of practice with critical teachers/researchers working to interrupt these relations through critical curriculum and teach-ing practices.

After the work with the students, the discussions in the "Friday Semi-nar" that Michael holds every week with his graduate students and with re-searchers and activists who had come to spend time with him were no less socially and educationally critical than before (see Apple 2000), but some-thing had changed: they became more grounded. The theories and critical research we were developing were now linked to the experiences of the seventh-grade students. This was not simply rhetorical, as in "how would this help those students?" Rather, the students' multiple realities, diverse backgrounds, and questions became an impetus to the work we were com-mitted to already—connecting elegant theories and substantive research agendas to the lives of people in real institutions and real communities. The experiences in the classroom made it not only more compelling but also easier not to remain "on the balcony" (Apple 1999).

For example, intense discussions about the role of education in the re-production of and resistance to dominant ideological and economic forms took up issues of identity and "subject positions" more easily. This led to exceptionally interesting discussions on identity formation and the role of schooling in consistently providing alternative subject positions for stu-dents. Our ongoing deliberations about the tensions between neo-Marxist and postmodern/poststructural approaches were filtered through the real-ities of the students with whom we interacted. This produced a more nu-anced and grounded set of experiences that brought our group together across differences. For examples, doctoral students from other nations were able to rethink their stereotypes of U.S. schooling. Just as important, the work enabled students from the United States—all of whom were very socially and culturally critical—to reconnect their critical analyses to a real vision of oppositional curricula and teaching. They connected substantive critique and committed counterhegemonic educational action in a more organic relation. This is something that Michael has stressed for years in opposition to the all-too-ethereal discourse that unfortunately dominates the literature on "critical pedagogy." The work with the classroom helped the graduate students develop an ongoing disposition to continue working in and on schools.

Building the Larger Coalition

The socially and pedagogically progressive curriculum design that lies at the heart of the project described here is the result of a longer and wider chain of collaborative efforts. Barbara and others had already been involved in ongoing collaborative efforts between another university professor and several middle school teachers. This group had numerous conversations about the distressing realities of education and the less-than-engaging school experiences they were observing. Feeling frustrated by what was not happening even in their classrooms, the small group of educators decided to act proactively to change the status quo. Using the work of James Beane (1993), a professor at National-Louis University and coeditor with Michael of *Democratic Schools*, they created a way for students and teachers to plan the curriculum collaboratively. This approach was first used in a unit called "Living in the Future" (Brodhagen, Weilbacher, and Beane 1998). Jim became a frequent member of the team and participated in daily planning sessions, teaching classes, organizing activities, correcting work, going on field trips, and building relationships with students. Curriculum conversations occurred on a daily basis among both school- and university-based participants to think through the creation of a classroom where there was legitimate discourse about important things between and among students and teachers.

It was these efforts that also ultimately led to Michael and his group's participation. While the seeds of curriculum integration took root in this classroom, Jim (an active participant in the Friday Seminar for many years) described what was happening to Michael and the other educators working with him. He reported how students wrote a classroom constitution and conducted self-evaluations, writing goals, creating portfolios, and learning how to run a student–parent–teacher conference. The group of university-based educators and researchers discussed issues arising from students' questions about the self and the world and about current events on a regular basis. Graduate students and some professors who supported these curricular efforts began to collaborate with the teachers. To Michael, Jim's description and Michael's ongoing work with Barbara on things such as the history of democratic and socially critical curriculum and teaching made this a test case of whether challenges to dominant curricular knowledge and processes could be built, defended, and made to last. Given Michael's respect for Barbara, it was clear that something had to be given back, something that the teachers and students in that classroom had also made clear: that observers could not simply observe and had to give something meaningful back to their classroom.

As more university-based educators heard about this new experience, many graduate students requested to come and see what was happening. This interest may have been fueled by a sense of disbelief: could these kinds of curricular and pedagogical models actually be implemented, especially in a time of increasing dominance by conservative political positions in education and society at large? The growing interest may have resulted from the hope that concrete critical practices could be built to withstand conservative pressures while students could still do well on standardized tests, which were not going away anytime soon. The power of such hope must never be minimized.

Conclusion

The brief picture we have presented in this chapter cannot capture the complexities of the work we describe. The "Show Me the Money" theme included opportunities for students to do research with current economic data, historical information, Internet research, and conventional books. Students took field trips into communities, conducted simulations, and used multiple forms of media. They brought people from the community into the classroom, including, as we saw, people from the university who were willing to share particular areas of expertise or collaborate under the leadership of the students and the teachers. This in itself is worth noting, as is the impact that engaging with Barbara and her students had on the discourse and dispositions of critically oriented graduate students.

A vision of collaborative work in the service of critical social and educational understandings underpins the work of teachers such as Barbara who continually question why they must pursue tasks that have negative effects and are simply boring for students and teachers. This vision is embodied in the following personal statement by Barbara, which we feel is a clear summary of how the processes we have described in this chapter are situated in the larger personal, political, and pedagogic project of building an education worthy of its name:

> It has never occurred to me not to collaborate; it has always been a part of who I am as an educator. Doing curriculum integration requires that those involved collaborate. As a doctoral student who was also a middle school teacher doing this "cutting edge" democratic and progressive middle school curriculum work, my practice was made public to my peers in a very visible manner. There were videos, articles, and chapters being produced and written with numerous references to my work. I was talking about my teaching and writing papers in graduate classes at an institution that is known for its progressive faculty. I went there because I knew there would be like-minded professors who would support, but at the same time challenge, my teaching. The academic and professional collaboration questioned, challenged, and pushed my teaching to a different level.
>
> Early readings of the work of radical curriculum theorists and teachers challenged me to include issues relating to race, gender, and class in my teaching. Like many, I sought out works of literature by women and people of color. I tried to ask questions of my students that would challenge them to think about their position in the world relative to who they were. I was making progress. But when my teaching became public, questions were asked, not to judge, but to learn and to understand. Why did I say what I did to a young African American male? Did I think about the incredible range of family structures when I asked students to talk to family members? Aren't you manipulating students into doing what is already decided? Questions like these created dissonance for me, and I had to rethink some of what I thought I believed. The questioners were trying to fully understand what they saw or what I said was happening, and I in response wanted to be clear about my teaching. All of us were after a similar goal: to create radical, democratic, progressive teaching and learning experiences.
>
> Collaboration requires that two or more work jointly on a project even though the project may sometimes seem an unreachable goal. Some of my professors, fellow graduate students, and other progressive educators didn't

have a clear picture of what a radical, democratic progressive education in the late twentieth and early twenty-first century might look like. An idea came to life in the classroom where I was teaching, one that held real promise for so many young adolescents. By telling the story of our classroom and others like it, it was possible to articulate what a classroom could be like, one where the knowledge brought by students and produced by students was valued as much as knowledge from "experts." It is a classroom where the experiences of all bring richness to the questions, concepts, and themes that make up the curriculum. The teaching and learning in our classroom allowed a special kind of collaboration to occur.

While we believe that this kind of collaboration would find supporters among many teachers throughout the world, neither of us is romantic about the impact one teacher can have on social change in and through education. Yet education is not divorced from society; it is a significant *part* of society. Struggling through education—over its curriculum and pedagogy, over its goals, and over the rights of students to collaborate with others— *is* struggling in society. This perspective became clearer for people from the university as they helped build critical practice under the leadership of critically reflective teachers. For those of us who believe that a democratic and socially critical education can and must be built, this one small effort to engage in such collaboration and the effects it had on the participants may indeed be small. But let us imagine if it were multiplied a thousandfold. Now lets *do* it!

References

Apple, M. 1995. *Education and power.* New York: Routledge.

———. 1996. *Cultural politics and education.* New York: Teachers College Press.

———. 1999. *Power, meaning, and identity.* New York: Peter Lang.

———. 2000. *Official knowledge: Democratic education in a conservative age.* 2nd ed. New York: Routledge.

———. 2001. *Educating the "right" way: Markets, standards, God, and inequality.* New York: Routledge.

———. 2003. *The state and the politics of knowledge.* New York: Routledge.

Apple, M., and J. Beane, eds. 1995. *Democratic schools.* Alexandria, Va.: Association for Supervision and Curriculum Development.

Beane, J. 1993. *A middle school curriculum: From rhetoric to reality.* Rev. ed. Columbus, Ohio: National Middle School Association.

Brodhagen, B. 1995. The situation made us special. In *Democratic schools*, edited by M. Apple and J. Beane. Alexandria, Va.: Association for Supervision and Curriculum Development, 83–100.

Brodhagen, B., G. Weilbacher, and J. Beane. 1998. What we've learned from "Living in the future." In *The curriculum: Problems, politics, and possibilities*, 2nd ed., edited by M. Apple and L. Beyer. Albany: State University of New York Press, 117–33.

Building Hope: Implementing Unification Education in a South Korean Kindergarten

MINA KIM, INDIANA UNIVERSITY
SOO RYEON LEE, CHUN-CHUN PUBLIC KINDERGARTEN, SUWON, SOUTH KOREA

North and South Korea have been divided into two countries for over fifty years. For the first three decades after the Korean War, South Korean policies emphasized an anticommunist curriculum. Teachers and textbooks emphasized a "defeat Communism" education. School materials described North Koreans as having animal appearances, like pigs and wolves. Directly at school and indirectly through press reports and informal conversations, students were exposed to negative representations of North Korea.

As the century progressed, the tide turned, and authorities exerted less control over the North Korean images that South Korean children consumed inside and, for the most part, outside the classroom. In 1997, the president of South Korea, Kim Dae Jung, announced the "Sunshine Policy" toward North Korea. This initiative sought to foster dialogue through cultural and economic exchange and support between the two countries. As part of these new policies, the South Korean Ministry of Education began to emphasize a curriculum that presented North Koreans as part of the same national community rather than portraying them as an enemy with a different political ideology. Despite these efforts, young children, in particular, have few and often inaccurate ideas about North Korea and its people. Our experience as early childhood teachers, in fact, has been that many children appear to be literally uninterested in North Korea.

Although the Ministry of Education has emphasized unification education since the early 1990s, it is not yet an integral part of many classrooms (Ji and Kim 1998; Nou 2000; Yoon and Lee 1995). Studies suggest that teachers do not apply unification education in part because of a lack of teaching materials, shortness of time in their school day for new curricula, little familiarity with North Korean culture, and few tools for teaching about unification (Ji and Kim 1998; Yoon and Lee 1995). Moreover, many teachers lack a clear understanding of the historical and political context for both the separation and the unification of Korea (Nou 2000; Su and Jo 1995). Nonetheless, according to a 1998 survey, preschool teachers recognize the importance of unification education for young children and agree that it should be a part of the curriculum (Ji and Kim 1998). Teachers acknowledge their own confusion and lack of understanding about what unification education should look like and insist on the need for developing clear curricular tools. However, they seem to be waiting for others to develop this unification curriculum.

Given that teachers know the most about their own teaching and their own students, we began the collaboration described here by questioning why teachers appear to be waiting for someone else. Teachers, we believe, have the expertise and know-how to make a unification curriculum practical and to implement it in their classrooms. Here, we trace the experience of an accomplished public kindergarten teacher, Soo Ryeon, with implementing a unification curriculum through collaboration and dialogue with Mina Kim, a graduate student in early childhood education. We describe our emerging theoretical understanding of unification education and share Soo Ryeon's work implementing a unification curriculum.

When we began our collaborative exchange, the challenges of implementing a unification curriculum quickly became clear. Neither of us had ever incorporated unification, and Soo Ryeon already had a fixed curriculum for the month that did not include unification education. The practical obstacles she listed practically reflected earlier research findings. First, as she had already developed each month's curriculum, it was hard to schedule time for lessons related to unification. Second, she had no teaching materials related to unification. Third, because unification in South Korea included political and ideological concepts, it was unclear how she would address such controversial concepts with young children. Finally, although required by the South Korean Ministry of Education, there seemed to be no clear reasons why unification should be covered in kindergarten settings. While these were tangible challenges, they did not seem like compelling reasons to deprive young children of a chance to learn about unification and about their northern neighbors. In fact, we felt that it was awkward not to mention North Korea in the curriculum since teaching units like "World and Other Countries" have become common in South Korean kindergartens.

Soo Ryeon decided to participate in Mina's research by developing and implementing unification education. Because of the distance, Soo Ryeon implemented these unification activities without Mina's direct help. However, we collaborated closely through photographs and written reflections. Through sharing ideas about creative, developmentally appropriate ways to teach complex subjects to very young children, we hoped to discover an effective way for realizing unification education. For five months, we sought to understand the unification of North and South Korea. Did we, in fact, need unification education in early childhood, and what were reasons not to apply unification education? We also investigated some of the constraints of using a unification curriculum in kindergarten classrooms. We concluded that unification education not only deals with Korea's tragic situation but also is a way to introduce concepts of peace and cooperation, which are greatly valued in early childhood settings.

Unification, Peace Education, and Early Childhood

Nou (2000) defines unification education as an educational program for young generations to contribute to the reunification of a divided country. According to the Ministry of Education of the Republic of South Korea (1993), unification education emphasizes the similarities between North and South Koreans as it prepares citizens for a unified country built on ideals of freedom, social welfare, and democracy. From this perspective, learning to resolve conflicts within the constraints of community law and with respect for the rights of the individual is central to learning about responsible citizenship.

If the ultimate goal of unifying South and North Korea is to regain a concept of national community, early childhood is a critical period (Yoon and Lee 1995). In early education, unification education does not emphasize the political meanings of unification but tends to stress embracing North Korea as part of the same national community. Therefore, some scholars in South Korea believe that unification education should offer opportunities for young children to construct a sense of active participation in a democratic society (Lee 2000; Nou 2000). Yoon and Lee (1995) suggest three approaches: the direct unification education approach, the democracy civic education approach, and the peace education approach. The South Korean Ministry of Education advocates the third.

In many respects, implementing unification education in kindergarten classrooms is similar to teaching about peace, conflict resolution, cooperation, nonviolence, and social responsibility. While unification education is unique to "divided" countries—countries separated by distinctive political agendas and war—the goal in South Korea is to engage all citizens in reunification efforts and prepare them for future democratic citizenship. Thus, the fundamental concepts of unification education are related to peace and democratic education. While many South Korean teachers, like Soo Ryeon, may be unfamiliar with the concept of democratic/peace education and how to apply it in early childhood education, the framework of peace education is a useful tool for articulating the broad goals of a unification curriculum.

Peace education for young children creates humane, nonviolent learning environments (Stomfay-Stitz and Hinitz 1998). In other countries, children are taught about conflict resolution, economic well-being, political participation, and concern for the environment. Within the context of unification education in South Korea, peace education might include understanding different perspectives and lifestyles, cooperating and sharing, conflict resolution, noncompetitive measures, and civil interactions with others.

Peace education not only talks about the absence of war but also emphasizes appreciation of other people, a lifestyle of reconciliation, taking action to solve problems and resolve conflicts, and justice (Hinitz 1994). Early childhood education often stresses how to solve conflicts, focuses on other cultures, fosters cooperation, and teaches respect for self and others in daily life. While these concepts were present in South Korean kindergartens, they had not been directly employed in unification education efforts. Implementing these overlapping concepts, therefore, would foster peace and democracy by relating them to the historical and political perspectives of North Korea and to the idea of reunification.

When talking about unification education, however, it is not immediately evident that it would include taking action to solve problems since children know so little about North Korea. Clearly, the people of South and North Korea have developed different political and social perspectives during the past two generations. However, without knowing much about North Korea, talking with children about reunification in the classroom would be difficult. We felt, therefore, that unification education in kindergarten should mention our political conditions and then draw peace and democratic educational themes from the unification curriculum. Talking about the separation of North and South Korea and explaining the history of and reasons for the split would lay a stronger foundation for teaching appreciation, taking actions to solve problems, and resolving conflicts within the unification curriculum. However, we did not want this to be a one-time introduction to North Korea. Rather, we sought to incorporate unification education within the standardized kindergarten curriculum, cultivating unification education as a type of peace and democratic early childhood education.

Applying a Culturally Relevant Child-Centered Curriculum

The largest initial obstacle in this work was the lack of unification teaching materials for young children. Most of the materials Soo Ryeon identified in South Korea were inappropriate for five-year-old children. Mina, however, found teaching materials about peace education for young children in the United States, many of which incorporated the arts (Schiller and Hastings 1998; Stomfay-Stitz and Hinitz 1998; Thompson 1995). She also identified research suggesting significant improvements of children's knowledge about peace through the use of artwork (J. H. Kim 1997; M. H. Kim 2001; Ministry of Education of the Republic of South Korea 2000).

Based on this, we decided to incorporate arts activities into our unification curriculum, focusing on three activities—storytelling, drawing a related picture, and writing poems—all common activities in Korean kindergarten classrooms. We framed the storytelling about North Korea and its people as an input activity, while we focused on expressive drawing and writing a poem as output activities. For the storytelling, as one example, we prepared a map of Korea to show how North and South were divided and to explain why. We also planned a "North Korean friend" activity for cooperative work in small groups to emphasize the peace concept.

The first challenge in implementing the curriculum emerged unexpectedly. Since these children had no idea about North Korea or unification, it was necessary to begin with activities such as guessing games. When asked about a place we cannot go within our country, the students offered answers such as "Underground!" "Heaven!" and "A cave under the sea!" Despite their fanciful responses, their lack of awareness about North Korea required a more direct approach. "We can go to many other countries except this country, although it is also part of ours. That is North Korea," Soo Ryeon explained awkwardly. The children looked confused. A few had heard about North Korea, but the majority did not know how the two countries were related and why they could not go to the North. As children sat listening attentively, she explained what happened on our peninsula many years ago. From this historical background, she described the current starvation in North Korea. "I will share my food with hungry North Korean friends," declared one child. Others chimed in, "I want to go to a mountain with North Korean friends to catch a leaf insect," and, "North Korean children and I will go to a supermarket to buy a meat to eat."

The children's ideas naturally connected to their drawings and their poems. We arranged several small groups and had the children discuss what they drew on one large sheet of paper. They seemed pleased to work collaboratively. Interestingly, some children said that they drew Russians who came with North Koreans to visit South Korea. Soo Ryeon explained the historical background, citing Russia, China, England, and the United States as supportive countries around the world. Their drawings suggested that the students had accepted North Korean children as new friends. They were also eager to participate in the poetry-writing activity and even required extra materials. Their poems about unification were displayed on the wall.

By the end of our collaboration, we were intrigued by the impact of this unification education unit. Next year, Soo Ryeon plans to teach unification curriculum for one week under the theme "Our Country" and "Our World." She will also involve children's parents to help search for material and enhance interest in unification. She will still include storytelling with a Korean map of Korea and reading books about North Korea. The children will further explore differences between North and South Korea in cultures, language, and foods; make a small North Korean dictionary; and listen to North Korean songs. The curriculum will also underscore the two countries' similarities, and students will draw small maps of a unified Korea in small groups, write a letter to North Korean friends, and create poems and cooperative pictures.

Through our engagement in unification education, we concluded that creative teachers, with support, can develop a meaningful curriculum drawing on their personal and practical knowledge about their students. For Mina, working with Soo Ryeon provided the opportunity to understand how a preschool teacher accepted unification education and implemented it in a classroom setting. For Soo Ryeon, the collaboration provided her with the theoretical and empirical knowledge to inform her work and develop new ideas. Our collaboration illustrates how theory and practice can be combined and carried out when researchers and teachers work together— even from great distances. More important, through this work we addressed our sense of responsibility for our children's initial disinterest in unification and in North Korea. Through these activities, the children showed great interest in the stories and paid attention to the historical and political explanations. They participated in the activities and enjoyed them, confirming the importance of providing an initial exposure to North Korea and unification to the kindergartners.

Conclusion

The notion that North Korea has a plan to develop nuclear weapons has aroused the public interest and raised controversy. The U.S. media often report that the matter of North Korea is dangerous and that its leaders are unforgivable. Since the Bush administration included North Korea in the "Axis of Evil," this country is perceived, particularly in the United States, as a serious international problem. However, the majority of South Koreans believe that casting North Korea in such a light has created unnecessary tensions between South and North and has interfered with their desire for Korean unification (Brooke 2002).

Despite earlier conflicts, many South Koreans consider North Koreans as family; there are many South Korean people who have parents, siblings, and kin living in North Korea, and in 2000, South and North Korea cooperated in the first family reunion at Seoul and Pyongyang. Uniting family members separated by the Korean War was given top priority at the historic summit meeting between South Korean President Kim Dae Jung and North Korean leader Kim Jong Il in June 2000 (Strom 2000). Afterward, a newspaper poll showed that younger South Koreans changed their opinion of reunification from negative to positive; seven out of ten junior high and high school students were hopeful about reunification and an equal ratio of college-educated South Koreans endorsed reunification (Jang 2002; H. J. Kim 2000). Even the American press has acknowledged that the younger South Korean generation does not believe that North Korea will use weapons against them and that South Koreans have a positive view of South Korea's Sunshine Policy (Brooke 2002).

South Koreans have been concerned about their relations with North Korea and have been hoping for a long time to move toward unification. This is not an impromptu passion but rather a long-cherished desire. At his inauguration ceremony, South Korean President Roh Moo Hyun announced his North Korea policy as "Peace-Prosperity Policy." Although he rejects North Korea's nuclear development, his policy toward North Korea remains similar to the Sunshine Policy of the prior administration. South Korea will continue to engage North Korea economically and politically toward reunification (C. K. Kim 2003).

Despite the current divisions in the sociopolitical globalized world, we believe that unification education is necessary, especially for young Korean children who will eventually hold the reins of reunification. Thus, these young children need democracy and peace education to develop a sense of community in classrooms and schools toward fulfilling dreams for reunification as well as democratic and peaceful interactions between the two nations. Whether in eastern Europe, the Middle East, or Korea, turbulence creates a global necessity for unification and peace education. Educating democratic citizens who have an awareness of self and community and of conflict resolution and problem solving, as well as a love of nature and social inclusiveness, begins in the early years.

References

Brooke, J. 2002. In Seoul, longing for the North. *New York Times*, December 22, 4.

Hinitz, B. 1994. Early childhood education for peace. In *Resources for early childhood: A handbook*, edited by H. Nuba, M. Searson, and D. L. Sheiman. New York: Garland, 249–86.

Jang, Y. E. 2002. Youth 65%, we should use the North Korean flag. *Yonhapnews*, August 21. www3.yonhapnews.net/cgi-bin/naver/getnews?042002082101200+20020821+0901 (accessed June 6, 2003).

Ji, S. A., and S. J. Kim. 1998. A study of early childhood education in South, North Korea in preparation for reunification. *Early Childhood Education Study* 18(2): 25–50.

Kim, C. K. 2003. The president Roh takes office as president. *Hankyoreh Daily Newspaper*, February 24. www.hani.co.kr/section-003000000/2003/02/003000000200302241914125.html (accessed June 6, 2003).

Kim, H. J. 2000. Younger generation, different point of view about unification. *Hankyoreh Daily Newspaper*, July 20. www.hani.co.kr/section-005000000/2000/005000000200007202331021.html (accessed June 6, 2003).

Kim, J. H. 1997. The effect of story books on young children's peace concept. Master's thesis, Chungang University.

Kim, M. H. 2001. The effect of activities for Korean unification on children's recognition toward North Korea. Master's thesis, Kwang-Ju University.

Lee, M. H. 2000. The way of exploration toward education for unification in early childhood education. *Journal of Future Early Childhood Education* 7(2): 361–90.

Ministry of Education of the Republic of South Korea. 1993. *The manual for teaching unification education*. Seoul: Ministry of Education.

———. 2000. *Teaching materials of activities for kindergartners*. Seoul: Ministry of Education.

Nou, M. J. 2000. A study on the reality of teacher cognition and direction of unification education in kindergarten. Master's thesis, Chongshin University.

Schiller, S., and K. Hastings. 1998. *The complete resource book: An early childhood curriculum*. Beltsville, Md.: Gryphon House.

Stomfay-Stitz, A. M., and B. F. Hinitz. 1998. Integration of peace education conflict resolution with the arts and humanities: A new agenda for a new century. Paper presented at the Annual Conference of the Eastern Educational Research Association, Tampa, Florida, February 1998 (ERIC Document Reproduction Service No. ED 421 226).

Strom, S. 2000. Foreign desk: Koreans, divided by war, await loved ones' return. *New York Times*, August 13. http://query.nytimes.com/gst/abstract.html?res=F60816FC385B0C708DDDA10894D8404482 (accessed June 6, 2003).

Su, K. S., and K. H. Jo. 1995. An analysis of the curriculum and text of our kindergarten education for unification in Korea. *Seowon University Educational Development* 14: 131–53.

Thompson, C. M. 1995. *The visual arts and early childhood learning*. Reston, Va.: National Art Education Association.

Yoon, K. Y., and M. S. Lee. 1995. A study of a kindergarten education plan for reunification in Korea. *Early Childhood Education Study* 15(1): 59–77.

Educating the Artist of the Future: Facing the   5
Challenge of Public Arts High Schools

ANNE R. CLARK, BOSTON ARTS ACADEMY, BOSTON,
   MASSACHUSETTS
RUBÉN A. GAZTAMBIDE-FERNÁNDEZ, HARVARD GRADUATE
   SCHOOL OF EDUCATION

Public arts high schools have proliferated throughout the United States, as evidenced by the growing membership of organizations such as the International Network of Performing and Visual Arts Schools. The mounting support for these specialized schools may indicate that despite U.S. public ambivalence toward the arts in education (Efland 1990), governmental and other cultural organizations have an interest in the education and training of young artists. Less clear is whether the goal of such institutions is to prepare young artists to assume a role as cultural workers or to provide alternative educational opportunities to a portion of the student population. The lack of a broad discourse about the public role of arts high schools is paralleled by the absence of scholarship about such schools.

While many researchers and scholars have paid special attention to the role of the arts in education (Efland 1990; Greene 1995; Siegesmund 1998), few have considered the particular challenges and opportunities of public arts high schools (Nathan 2003). Nonetheless, as public institutions accountable to the broader social and political context, public arts high schools—and the educators committed to them—must clearly articulate their purposes and goals. This is especially important in the context of standards-based reforms and testing, where the emphasis on academic preparation challenges how public arts high schools go about their business of training and educating young artists. Without explicit ideas about what public roles and responsibilities young artists should assume in a democratic society, these schools miss an opportunity to affirm their unique role as public institutions. Furthermore, as we will argue, clear goals as to the social roles of young artists provide a stronger basis for the resolution of curricular challenges in "artistic education" (Gaztambide-Fernández 2003).

We ground this chapter on our experiences at the Boston Arts Academy (BAA), the city's first public high school for the visual and performing arts. The academy is committed "to a rigorous academic and arts education for students who are eager to think creatively and independently, to question, and to take risks within a college preparatory program," as articulated in its mission statement. Throughout BAA's five-year history, some of the complications inherent in that mission have surfaced (Nathan 2002b). As practitioners of artistic education, the BAA's faculty have struggled with mixed messages about why arts education should exist and how it should be taught. These messages, revolving around the relationship between the arts and academic disciplines, create tensions rooted in different pedagogical beliefs and curricular understandings.

During our extended conversations in which we sought to explore these messages while bridging theory and practice, each of us had a unique perspective. Anne has been the curriculum coordinator and a humanities teacher at the BAA since the school was established in 1998. Part administrator and part teacher, she has been a participant in all discussions of school vision and practice. Rubén is a doctoral student, and in 2001, he researched the educational practices at the BAA as part of the Arts in Education Portraiture Project (Gaztambide-Fernández 2001). While conducting this research, we began our conversation regarding the ways in which curriculum theory could inform the particular challenges confronted by BAA faculty. Our conversation expanded into the broader challenges that public arts high schools faced—from issues of pedagogy to the politics of cultural production—and continually returned to the same question: to what end?

Addressing the educational challenges of public arts high schools requires a rationale, particularly in terms of defining the public roles that we envision for the young artists with whom we work. Here we argue that the focus of artistic education has been traditionally misplaced by insisting on distinctions between the arts and their academic counterparts. Instead, we believe our focus should be on the kinds of education that will prepare young artists to fulfill particular roles. In preparing youth to fulfill their role as artists within a social and political context, the close relationship between the arts and academic disciplines—and the ways in which both inform and support each other—emerges as a strength rather than a source of conflict and division.

Negotiating Arts and Academics: Toward a Unified Vision for the Educated Artist

When talking about the arts in education, the relationship between the arts and academic achievement is inescapable. Although a range of arguments have been made for the role of the arts in education (Siegesmund 1998), the notion that the arts support academic achievement remains one of the most compelling; an extensive body of research on arts education has focused on this relationship (Burton, Horowitz, and Abeles 2000; Catterall and Waldorf 1999). Nonetheless, as with most educational research, there are contradicting findings regarding this claim. A meta-analysis of quantitative studies on this issue, for example, suggests that such "instrumental claims" have weak empirical support (Winner and Hetland 2001). Furthermore, the authors argue it is misguided to advocate for the arts in education based on whether the arts support academic achievement, as it relegates the arts to an adjunct position in the curriculum. While this argument may have some merit, it ignores the political and social context in which arts education takes place.

Like all public schools, arts high schools are expected to meet the state's criteria for academic achievement—with all the pressures that entails (Nathan 2002a). Presumably, in an arts high school the arts are more than a curricular add-on. BAA faculty have worked hard to maintain the integrity of our arts programs despite increasing demands on our academic curriculum from high-stakes standardized testing. Since our students are also expected to demonstrate proficiency in the arts, arts training is not just a luxury that can be discarded so that more funding can go into testing preparation. Nonetheless, in response to public pressure, the temptation remains to argue that the arts improve academic achievement. More challenging, but ultimately more fruitful at the BAA, has been to connect arts to academics not because one can serve the other but because our students ultimately benefit from such an approach as both students and artists.

In practice, the cognitive relationship between arts and academic disciplines offers important opportunities for strengthening the overall curriculum. For example, responding to a disproportionate number of visual arts students struggling in math, BAA faculty incorporated animation and graphic design into the core math curriculum. Math teachers experimented with teaching series and patterns through animation and geometry in visually oriented units, resulting in higher student achievement in math. There are many plausible explanations for this, but what is crucial is that the approach was not to find a way to *use* visual arts to teach math but, rather, to *teach* math to visual artists—to draw on their artistic skills and strengths to teach them math. In turn, students also learned how to apply math concepts to their artistic work, which, we might presume, may have improved their craft. Rather than visual arts serving the needs of mathematics, math and visual arts informed each other. It is also possible that students were more committed and interested in the math curriculum because they were also improving their arts skills. Such an affective response suggests that arts high schools might first draw students who are committed to their artistic work and then school them in academics. Oddly, when we have taken an affective approach by using artistic interest as a point of leverage for getting students to work harder on their academics, we have been unsuccessful.

In the first few years of the school, we experimented with an "eligibility list," a concept borrowed from our district's athletic eligibility policy. Students needed to maintain a certain academic grade point in order to perform or show their work. Rather than spurring a new academic rigor, however, this approach resulted only in more and more students missing fundamental pieces of their artistic education. Ultimately, we found this approach contradicting; we do not pull students out of the science fair when they fail math, so why drop students from the choreography showcase when they do poorly in biology? In fact, we were undercutting the message of arts as a discipline by underscoring distinctions between the arts and academics.

In practice, we have been more successful in overall achievement by insisting that students respect the integrity of their arts disciplines and embrace their academic dimensions. We now require students to maintain a certain grade point on their arts course work in order to remain in the school. Encouraging students to understand the imbricate nature of artistic and academic disciplines foments an artistic seriousness of purpose that appears to carry over to the academic disciplines. Students have a stronger affective connection to their schooling when they understand how it fits within *their* visions as future artists. The promise of rigorous engagement in the arts and high expectations of their artistic work includes rather than elides a commitment to academic work.

When students have an affective connection to their schooling, they are more likely to engage, even in the aspects of school that at first seem least relevant to their commitments. Public arts high schools might provide the context for a renewed commitment to learning, one that is based not on what the state determines students should know and be able to do for an exam but rather on the students' personal commitments, passions, and desires. Furthermore, in the context of urban schools, it is especially equivocal to think of arts and academics as separate entities. This separation underscores artificial distinctions between students' artistic passions and commitments and their academic motivations—or lack thereof. When the whole of artistic education is framed as being both artistic and academic, students understand the role of both disciplines for their larger artistic purpose rather than as a competition between their passions and their deficits.

A Different View of Talent

At a recent arts high schools conference, a presenter from another school expressed an often-heard mantra among arts high schools: "I tell the students and their parents [during the application process] if they have the arts, I can get them the smarts. But if they don't have the arts, I can't help them." While elementary arts educators, following arts advocates from Dewey (1980) to Davis (1996), stress the artist in all of us, secondary educators tend to talk about students as if they had artistic talents or did not. This view resonates with the public imagination about artists and is reinforced by popular culture and through public debates about the role of the artist (Becker 2002; Gaztambide-Fernández 2002, 2003).

This, however, is a troubling claim for the academic faculty at BAA. We would never say, "Pedro will never be a scientist," and yet we try to give Pedro the best science education we possibly can, not only because it is mandated by the state but also because we believe, as educators, that it is our public moral responsibility. Artistic faculty, however, seem to feel more justified (and more comfortable) saying, "Pedro will never be a dancer." In the school context, this fundamental difference of belief causes innumerable tensions. When a student is not admitted or when a student is admitted yet does not succeed, academic and artistic faculty view and thus often initially approach the situation very differently.

Teachers of academic subjects, exposed to the role of race, class, and gender in schools in their teacher education programs, often question notions of talent and express skepticism that some students have more "natural talent" than others. BAA teachers, in particular, are aware of the trappings of tracking as a way of marginalizing students of color (Oakes 1985). Unfortunately, the great majority of undergraduate as well as graduate programs in the arts, including arts education and especially in disciplines such as music and dance, pay little or no attention to the social dimensions of artistic work (Becker 1989; Gaztambide-Fernández 2002). The image of the talented genius is largely unquestioned in the arts and informs the way that arts educators approach their work. In this sense, arts education remains largely undertheorized—well behind developments in pedagogical and curriculum theory (such as Pinar et al. 1995). Paradoxically, the arts play a crucial role in many of these scholars' theoretical writings and are embraced by many advocates for an education committed to social change (Collins 1993; Daspit and Weaver 1999; Giroux 1992; Poetter 2002).

BAA faculty have worked to bridge this tension in the realm of assessment. Ironically, arts teachers, inclined toward more rigid modes of instruction (tracking being the clearest example), are uncomfortable articulating artistic achievement through the rigid language of standards. They tend to see standards as a political necessity, something they need to create in response to demands from politicians. When they talk about assessment in the arts, it is about individual development, not generic benchmarks. In our experience, academic and artistic educators are more likely to employ deficit models when students do not come with this or that academic skill or cannot reach general benchmarks of academic proficiency. But when both sets of educators talk about the arts, they use a nurturance model. The artistic talk focuses on individualized models of growth rather than generic, standardized ones. This conversation is further complicated because the test of the Massachusetts Comprehensive Assessment System (MCAS), like most standardized tests, ignores artistic curricula—one-half of our school program! Needless to say, we have not found the standards-based approach, as presented by the MCAS exam, helpful. More productive has been our schoolwide portfolio system and a set of school-specific benchmarks that include both artistic and academic achievements.

At the heart of this tension is what we believe should be the public role of the artist and the kind of public education that will prepare them best to fulfill that role. Public arts high schools cannot escape this challenge, in great part because their public status confers on them the responsibility to make sure that the artists they graduate assume a public role. Public arts high schools cannot be content to use the arts to reach state-mandated academic standards, although that must certainly be a central goal. On the other hand, such schools have a public moral responsibility not to reproduce the traditional, elitist, and classist views of the artist (Gaztambide-Fernández 2003) and to permit private values and individualist views of talent to be funded by public resources.

Toward a More Useful Model

There is little agreement about the nature of artistic work and the role of the artist in society. As social subjects, artists and their work are shaped by their sociohistorical context (Becker 1994; Becker and Wiens 1995; Wolff 1993). Young artists receive a plethora of messages about their role as artists not only from the media and public debates but also from their teachers and from the curriculum that shapes their artistic educational experiences. When these messages enter the institutional context of the school, they result in a complicated and often contentious dialogue among educators. Tensions are particularly pronounced in the context of public arts high schools, where the search for an intellectual and empirical basis for arts education translates into mixed messages as to how and why young artists should be educated at the public's expense.

In every instance, the challenges discussed here have had at their core a perceived separation between the arts and academics. But such separation is neither natural nor essential. It is rooted in a set of myths and discourses that have become accepted as common sense (Feldman 1982; Gaztambide-Fernández 2003; Soussloff 1997; Wittkower and Wittkower 1963). There is a similar dichotomous view of the role of the artist and art in the public and private domains. Giroux (1995) observes that "artists have been caught in an ideological whirlwind regarding the role they play in their appeal to a wider public" (4). Reflecting on West's (1990) description of the "significant shift in the sensibilities and outlooks of critics and artists"

(19), some arts-in-education scholars argue that a curriculum must include a range of conceptions of the artist and the disparate roles artists play in the broader social context (Freedman and Hernández 1998; Garber 1995; Gaztambide-Fernández 2003; Neperud 1995).

More than being in a unique position to address this challenge, public arts high schools have a public and moral responsibility to think carefully about what kinds of artists they will educate. Experiences at the BAA have led teachers to focus less on the tension between arts and academics and more on our work to support student artists as cultural workers contributing to a vibrant democratic society. Because this requires that students understand the fundamental relationship between arts and academics, we have been able to better address the demands of state-mandated standards by making the most of the cognitive and affective responses discussed in this chapter. Meanwhile, in response to our public role, we have embraced the political dimensions of artistic work.

The Senior Grant Proposal is the culmination of this artistic and academic vision. BAA seniors identify a community need and propose an artistic project to address it in a rigorous grant format (complete with research and projected budget). On what we call "The Big Night," community members and actual grants administrators from Boston area foundations listen as students present their proposals. To date, about ten out of some one hundred seniors have each received around $500 in projects grants. Students who complete these grant projects also receive special accolades at graduation. Believing that a community is defined by what it celebrates, we designed this capstone project to celebrate the kinds of artists we wanted to graduate into the world: artists who are academically well prepared (able to research, write, and quantify), artistically proficient (able to present and implement their artistic visions), and civic minded (able to creatively address the needs they recognize in their communities through their artistic work).

References

Becker, C. 1989. Art students require a truly rigorous core curriculum, to help them develop intellectually as well as artistically. *Chronicle of Higher Education*, June 21, B1–B2.

———. 2002. *Surpassing the spectacle: Global transformations and the changing politics of art.* Lanham, Md.: Rowman & Littlefield.

———, ed. 1994. *The subversive imagination.* New York: Routledge.

Becker, C., and A. Wiens, eds. 1995. *The artist in society: Roles, rights, and responsibilities.* Chicago: New Art Examiner.

Burton, J., R. Horowitz, and H. Abeles. 2000. Learning in and through the arts: The question of transfer. *Studies in Art Education* 41(3): 228–57.

Catterall, J. S., and L. Waldorf. 1999. Chicago arts partnerships in education: Summary evaluation. In *Champions of change: The impact of the arts on learning,* edited by E. Fiske. Washington, D.C.: President's Committee on the Arts and Humanities, 47–62.

Collins, E. C. 1993. Special issue: Using the arts to inform teaching. *Theory into Practice* 32(4).

Daspit, T., and J. A. Weaver, eds. 1999. *Popular culture and critical pedagogy: Reading, constructing, connecting.* New York: Garland.

Davis, J. H. 1996. Why must we justify arts learning in terms of other disciplines? *Education Week,* October 16, 32, 34.

Dewey, J. 1980. *Art as experience.* New York: Perigee Books.

Efland, A. 1990. *A history of art education.* New York: Teachers College Press.

Feldman, E. B. 1982. *The artist.* Englewood Cliffs, N.J.: Prentice Hall.

Freedman, K., and F. Hernández, eds. 1998. *Curriculum, culture, and art education.* Albany: State University of New York Press.

Garber, E. 1995. Teaching art in the context of culture: A study in the borderlands. *Studies in Art Education* 36(4): 218–32.

Gaztambide-Fernández, R. A. 2001. Portrait of the Boston Arts Academy. In *Passion and industry: Schools that focus on the arts,* edited by J. Davis. Natick, Mass.: National Arts and Learning Foundation, 105–82.

———. 2002. (De)constructing art as a model/(re)constructing art as a possibility. In *(Re)visioning the democratic ideal,* edited by T. Poetter, K. W. Baptist, C. Higgins, C. Haerr, and M. Hayes. Troy, N.Y.: Educators International Press, 83–107.

———. 2003. The artist in society: Understandings, expectations, and curriculum implications. Paper presented at the annual meeting of the American Research Association, Chicago, April 22.

Giroux, H. A. 1992. *Border crossings: Cultural workers and the politics of education.* New York: Routledge.

———. 1995. Borderline artists, cultural workers, and the crisis of democracy. In *The artist in society: Rights, roles, and responsibilities,* edited by C. Becker and A. Wiens. Chicago: New Art Examiner, 4–14.

Greene, M. 1995. *Releasing the imagination.* San Francisco: Jossey-Bass.

Nathan, L. 2002a. The human face of the high-stakes testing story. *Phi Delta Kappan* 83(8): 595–600.

———. 2002b. Through the lens of art. *Educational Leadership* 60(2): 22–25.

————. 2003. Creating equity from the ground up. *Horace* 19(3). www.essentialschools.org/cs/resources/view/ces_res/298 (accessed October 20, 2003).

Neperud, R. W., ed. 1995. *Context, content and community in art education: Beyond postmodernism.* New York: Teachers College Press.

Oakes, J. 1985. *Keeping track: How schools structure inequality.* New Haven, Conn.: Yale University Press.

Pinar, W., P. Slattery, W. Reynolds, and P. Taubman. 1995. *Understanding curriculum.* New York: Peter Lang.

Poetter, T. 2002. Opening myself up to writing fiction. In *In (Ex)clusion: (Re)visioning the democratic ideal,* edited by T. Poetter, C. Haerr, M. Hayes, C. Higgins, and K. W. Baptist. Troy, N.Y.: Educators International Press, 1–12.

Siegesmund, R. 1998. Why do we teach art today? Conceptions of art education and their justification. *Studies in Art Education* 39(3): 197–214.

Soussloff, C. 1997. *The absolute artist: The historiography of a concept.* Minneapolis: University of Minnesota Press.

West, C. 1990. The new cultural politics of difference. In *Out there: Marginalization and contemporary culture,* edited by R. Ferguson, M. Gever, T. Minh-ha, and C. West. Cambridge, Mass., and New York: MIT Press and New Museum of Contemporary Art, 19–36.

Winner, E., and L. Hetland, eds. 2001. *Beyond the soundbite: Arts education and academic outcomes.* Los Angeles: Getty Center.

Wittkower, R., and M. Wittkower. 1963. *Born under Saturn. The character and conduct of artists: A documented history from antiquity to the French Revolution.* London: Weidenfeld and Nicolson.

Transformative Curriculum Leadership: Inspiring Democratic Inquiry Artistry

6

ROSEMARY GORNIK, SOUTH EUCLID-LYNDHURST CITY
   SCHOOLS, OHIO
JAMES HENDERSON, KENT STATE UNIVERSITY
MICHELLE D. THOMAS, KENT STATE UNIVERSITY

This chapter tells the story of the process of enacting transformative curriculum leadership practices in a midwestern school district. As we passionately work to develop a public trust for our professional judgment with colleagues, community members, and politicians, we experience the challenges of an internal change process. "One of the central challenges to [educators] in the postmodern age," observed Guskey and Huberman (1995) is "working within contexts of pervasive moral uncertainty" (15). As school leaders, how do we know we are challenging our inquiry capacities as well as the inquiry capacities of teachers, students, and leaders? Providing evidence to support our collective wisdom is the catalyst for pursuing a more general professional question: How can school leaders work collaboratively with teachers to maintain an interconnectedness of high standards, sophisticated decision making, ongoing professional inquiry, and student learning while embracing transformative practices?

The story of our K–12/university collaborative work begins with a series of meetings in the spring of 2000 to discuss the theoretical underpinnings of the reform effort. Our conversations centered on the distinction between "standards-based educational reform" and "curriculum-based educational reform." We recognized that standards-based reform was the dominant paradigm for school districts in this midwestern state—and throughout the United States. This paradigm is based on a very straightforward command-and-control logic associated with approaching education as an efficient business (Cuban 2003). During our conversations, we felt fortunate that this local school district was "winning" the standardized management game. Paradoxically, this provided the superintendent and the director of instruction and professional development in the district a certain freedom to move toward a new paradigm.

Theoretical Overview of the Reform Problem and Process

Curriculum-based educational reform is a multifaceted collaborative process comprised of eight interrelated dimensions conceptualized broadly as building inquiry capacity and building organizational capacity. Within a school district of twenty-four self-selected teachers and administrators, this *transformative curriculum leadership* reform effort sought to elevate professional judgments (Burns 1978)—specifically curriculum judgments. This, however, could occur only in a context of facilitating deep-seated personal, institutional, and cultural changes (Henderson and Hawthorne 2000). The individual dimensions of the reform process are presented in table 6.1.

Building a democratic platform is the first dimension in table 6.1. Informed by Schwab's (1978) practical essays, Walker (1971) identifies platform building as a key feature of curriculum deliberations. The curriculum developer begins with a system of beliefs and values that guides the task based upon "an idea of what is and a vision of what ought to be" (52). The platform construction positions curriculum workers in the democratic here-and-now (Dewey 1989). They must carefully consider how their educational services are, in very concrete ways, instances of democratic living. They must think about curriculum as a challenge to practice wise judgments (Henderson and Kesson 2003).

Dewey's (1963) *Experience and Education* informs the notion of "3S" learning, which refers to the integration of deep subject matter understanding with democratic self and social learning. The quality of the 3S platform deliberations is highly dependent on educators' inquiry capacities. This is, of course, a central point in Dewey's work.

Though educators may have a general feel for the command-and-control logic of standards-based educational reform, this is not the case for the inquiry logic of curriculum-based educational reform experienced in this local school district. In addition, making sound judgments with reference to the goodness of our lives involves a human psychological capacity (Kekes 1995). It may take a very sophisticated epistemological capacity (Kegan

Table 6.1. Transformative Curriculum Leadership

Dimension	Collaborative Process
Building inquiry capacity	
Building a democratic platform	Creating a curriculum platform that provides a coherent standpoint for facilitating a balanced "3S" education, referring to "deep" subject matter understanding integrated with democratic self and social learning. The intent is to position curriculum work as an exercise in practical wisdom.
Cultivating curriculum inquiry	Designing ways to cultivate the "arts of inquiry" associated with approaching curriculum work as an exercise in practical wisdom.
Creative designing	Creating unit designs informed by the platform decision making. This is the enactment of a visionary design process that links the platform construction with student learning assessment before moving to instructional planning.
Artistic, reflective teaching	Teaching the unit artistically. Enacting a creative reflection-in-practice and reflection-on-practice.
Building organizational capacity	
Comprehensive evaluation	Enacting a holistic formative and summative evaluation of the preceding dimensions.
Building a work culture	Practicing organizational development that nurtures a supportive work culture. This work has three interrelated components: trust building, critical assessment, and collaborative problem solving.
Cultivating public understanding	Practicing community development that cultivates public awareness and appreciation. This work focuses on creating an authentic public "space" for democratic education.
Establishing a network	Building a support system of transformative curriculum leaders by identifying interested curriculum stakeholders, supporting their transformative leadership efforts, and creating networking opportunities.

1982, 1994) to understand democratic values as a moral standard for conduct in the classroom (Gornik 2003; Henderson and Hawthorne 2000).

Our reform effort also necessitates comprehensive formative and summative evaluation because of the highly embedded nature of the eight collaborative dimensions. Furthermore, though individual educators may be able to practice many of these dimensions, their efforts will forever be at risk without a supportive work culture (Fullan and Hargreaves 1996; Sarason 1990). This is why building organizational capacity—with its interrelated trust building, critical assessment, and collaborative action phases (Schmuck and Runkel 1985)—is so important. Cultural change is impossible without the cultivation of a broad political base (Sergiovanni 1992, 2000; Walker 2003).

Throughout this two-year collaboration, working to facilitate deepseated personal, institutional, and cultural changes placed an enormous stress on individuals. If educators could not find ways to support one another, then their transformative efforts would fail.

Phase I: Constructing the Reform Problem

In phase I, the K–12/university collaborative focused on an overarching question: How can the district create an ethos for transformative professional development by exploring the interconnectedness of high standards facilitated as a balanced 3S platform and constructivist student learning, sophisticated curriculum decision making as an exercise in practical wisdom, and arts of professional inquiry? Using an action research framework, these twenty-four district curriculum workers became the Professional Development Process Team (PDPT). Participants could earn three university workshop credits for their year-long work, and each received a $1,500 stipend. Their journey began by meeting monthly during the school day, reflecting on their practices, exploring and selecting topics of interest, designing an inquiry-based professional curriculum leadership project, and performing research with guidance from colleagues and university professors.

Building Inquiry Capacity

Enacting these transformative dimensions in the democratic here-and-now (Dewey 1989) is highly dependent on the educators' inquiry capacities. To build this capacity, the PDPT began to develop a culture for professional growth by experimenting with cognitive coaching (Costa and Garmston 1994), examining teachers' inquiry artistry (Henderson 2001), and developing professional portfolios (Lyons 1998). As scaffolding for reflective teacher learning, teacher apprenticeship (Barton and Collins 1993; Loughran and Corrigan 1995), and educational leadership, the portfolios provided a venue to document the growth experiences. These centered on two questions:

1. How can the team develop standards for long-term growth and development of the educators in the district in connection with teaching, learning, and leadership?
2. How can the team establish and maintain an inquiry-based professional ethics through peer review and/or other collegial strategies?

The interplay of these organizing questions guided the growth and development of the team. To begin, cognitive coaching fostered professional collegiality, a deepening reflection, and a responsible autonomy (Costa and Garmston 1994). Furthermore, cognitive coaching invited participants to inquire about their practices rather than being informed about their practices through administrative reviews.

To further support this transformative process, Guild and Garger (1985) suggest that educators should become bicognitive: they need to learn to think in terms of continuous student and teacher learning. PDPT members contemplated how to invite continuous learning and practice cognitive coaching strategies as they explored forms of inquiry (Henderson 2001). Furthermore, in the context of cultivating their inquiry and reflective capacities, participants engaged in autobiographical reflection (philosophical introspection), collaborative reflection (asking questions and seeking answers beyond self), and communal reflection (self-reflection in interaction with others within larger contexts) (Rearick and Feldman 1999).

Educators possess different epistemological capacities (Kegan 1982, 1994); they have different talents and interests. Thus, it is critical to provide professional growth opportunities that give high priority to collegial conversation, provide for collaborative learning, and invite reflection (Darling-Hammond and McLaughlin 1995; Zepeda 1999). Human development viewed as an interactive process between the educator and the work environment is an important source for understanding individual capacity for transformative curriculum leadership.

Early on, team members expressed concerns about the readings being too "theory" oriented. 3S deliberation certainly requires the practice of sophisticated arts of inquiry in the spirit of Schwab's (1978) analysis of the eclectic arts of curriculum practice and Eisner's (1994) insights into the educational imagination, and these deliberations challenged the participants. Once engaged in discussions about the readings with colleagues and university faculty, many began to make personal, professional, and student connections. The nonthreatening milieu invited members to share their ideas, and monthly meetings provided valuable time to work, talk, and interact. One member enthusiastically pronounced, "The energy and enthusiasm in the room is contagious!" Another member expressed the importance of exploring self-selected personal and professional needs and interests rather than externally imposed directives.

PDPT members worked to develop their inquiry capacity by moving beyond the craft or technical side of teaching (Tom 1984) and leadership toward a more generative (self as lifelong learner) and generous (respect of human diversity) approach to teaching and leadership (Henderson 2001). For example, one team member changed "normal" in her department by developing a thematic approach to teaching foreign language. She stretched her students, as well as the members in the department, beyond rote memorization of vocabulary and the conjugation of verbs to a more deep and focused understanding of the language and the culture of the people.

Educators who value generativity provide high-level, thinking-centered, collaborative, problem-based learning environments. Furthermore, they modeled generosity as they interacted with students, colleagues, parents, and staff. These learning communities were supportive of the growth and development of all who participated.

Building Organizational Capacity

Encouraging cultures of collaboration (Fullan 1993) is an essential component to the longevity of such an initiative and in building inquiry capacity. Research suggests that educators who experience such a culture work collaboratively rather than in isolation and take more risks (Little 1987), commit to continuous rather than episodic improvement (Rosenholtz 1989), tend to be more caring with students and colleagues (Nias, Southworth, and Yeomans 1989; Taafaki 1992), are more assertive in relation to external pressures and demands (Hargreaves 1994), and experience greater opportunities to improve and learn from one another (Woods 1990). The K–12/university partnership allowed educators to establish a network and learn from each other on an ongoing basis.

Efforts to develop the district's organizational capacity were concentrated on communicating a compelling purpose, conducting a districtwide needs assessment, and development of action plans that would enact the compelling purpose. As might be expected, this work challenged the dominant management culture.

Productive Disequilibrium

As participants considered necessary changes representing major shifts in perspective and practice, they began to experience productive disequilibrium (Lord 1994). Further discord was prompted by the readings and the discussions as they struggled to make connections to practice. As a result, a conversation occurred that brought to light concerns, issues, and questions regarding the team's initiatives.

Initially, participants grappled with questions about maintaining teaching and leading responsibilities while working on this team. They wondered what they were trying to accomplish and how their success would be measured. Enacting a holistic formative and summative evaluation of their inquiry capacities, for example, is one very important and challenging dimension of transformative curriculum leadership. Participants wondered how a portfolio process for evaluation would impact the district, and they wrestled with questions about providing ongoing communication with colleagues and the broader community. To this point in the history of the district, evaluation of teachers consisted of clinical checklists and brief narratives developed by the administrator after a forty- to fifty-minute classroom observation. The prospect of a more collaborative portfolio process for teacher evaluation evoked concern in some members of the teachers' association.

Practicing organizational and community development that cultivates public awareness was difficult. Although additional administrative personnel assisted in developing the district's transformative leadership capacity, this dimension proved to be among the most challenging within this reform initiative.

As the work of the team progressed, action research questions designed by the participants such as, "What is the best way to provide support for teachers of elementary gifted students?" prompted them to move outside their comfort zones and, in a few cases, into unknown territories. In this case, each team member took a great professional risk with her colleagues in attempts to serve the needs of gifted students in the regular classroom. The prevailing culture of the school had been that gifted students could/would learn on their own. Her action research moved some beyond their limits, and she reported, "Doors were literally closed in my face" as a result.

Over time, members of the PDPT developed a mutual trust, supported the infusion of ideas, honored time for reflection and learning, and gained respect for individual differences. Team members were generous, contributing to the disequilibrium that generates energy for learning and for change. They also experienced challenges in moving beyond the "*How* do I practice?" to exploring and articulating "*What* do I practice and *why*?" and "*What* needs to be accomplished and *why*?"

Participants' professional leadership projects and portfolios provided evidence of their reflections on what they learned:

Chris's Reflections

The professional development process dramatically affected my perspective both professionally and personally. I experienced a range of emotions as I was engaged in critical inquiry. I must admit I did not like some of the answers I found, and that realization created the impetus to radically alter my frame of reference with respect to my professional and personal life. As a member of the PDPT, I read and reflected upon my current practices. As a small group of team members examined critical inquiry, one of the questions I raised was, "Why am I not doing what I feel needs to be done?" This was disheartening to me since I had always prided myself on doing what was right and fighting for what I believed. It concerned me that I had developed a complacent attitude with respect to feeling powerless to devoting the time necessary to bringing forth real change and, furthermore, at the level of perfection I expected in myself. I had always prided myself in my ability to do what I knew was right and to do it to the absolute best of my ability.

Kevin's Reflections

As a member of the PDPT, I was able to work through a process that invited committed teachers to work together to solve problems and to become even better teachers. I had a general idea of what inquiry-based thinking was about, and it made sense to me as I considered the reality that teachers are the ones who are best able to identify and address issues that arise in their classrooms. As a team member, I waded into the readings, which provided the background information and the theory behind what we were developing. At times, I felt overwhelmed and thought perhaps I was not going to grasp some of the complex concepts that were introduced. However, I kept coming back to what I saw as the core premise of the team: doing what is best for students, the community, and myself. I saw the team guiding me in the development of an inquiry framework that was intended to help me continue to grow and to develop as a teacher.

Phase II: Sustaining the Transformative Effort

By the end of phase I, the cohesion between and among the team members was palpable and measurable. However, the pressure to "go public" created a tremendous amount of stress on some members. This was due largely to work that could not be explained in a sentence or two. It was not a "sound bite"; it was not prescriptive. The connection to the university also was frightening to some.

Within the district, resistance became manifest in at least two ways. First, PDPT members experienced overt and covert criticism by nonparticipating faculty and staff. Second, the faculty at large resisted the change efforts of the PDPT, using the district's "excellent" rating with the state department of education as a cloak to maintain the status quo. Notions such as "If it is not broken, why fix it?" emerged.

The consequence of such resistance was apparent. Of the twenty-four educators on the team in the first year, only eight returned for the second year notwithstanding the powerful culture of team collaboration. While it is reasonable to assume that a variety of factors had an impact, cultivating public understanding of this work certainly created political pressure. Four teachers and four administrators now made up the team. The stipend was eliminated; however, university workshop credit remained an option, as did professional development units for teacher license renewal.

The superintendent, the director of instruction and professional development, and the university professors were cognizant of the personal and interpersonal aspects of such sophisticated work and recognized the structural and systemic changes required for its continuation. Working with the feedback, they created invitational opportunities that honored participants' developmental readiness for this challenging work.

In phase II, PDPT participants met monthly after school so as not to be out of their classrooms or buildings. Changes were made in the meeting format. There was more small-group and individual work, and each person was able to give input and lead the group. Members continued to work collaboratively on projects that had an impact in the buildings and/or across the district. (The district's professional development program grew out of this work and involved many of the faculty in the district who were not actually part of the team, despite professional and personal criticism.) Professional development opportunities continued to be offered, including professional readings, collaborative dialogue, written reflections, and curricular-related projects. By the end of phase II, however, it became increasingly clear that the wider culture could not or would not sustain the team's collaborative and transformative approach to teaching and leadership. By June of the second year, the superintendent and the director of instruction and professional development left the district; the PDPT dissolved.

Resistance, Relevance, Readiness

Personal readiness lies at the heart of the call to practical wisdom (Gornik 2003), and an educator's equilibrium is often maintained by being in alignment with the values created by the school environment (Eisner 1994). Teachers adopting this kind of visionary curriculum practice will find themselves in conflict with management-controlled curriculum implementation. In this reform effort, PDPT members could not or would not function outside the accepted values of the wider school culture. For example, one member noted that teachers lost interest after the first year because "inquiry was not a natural thing for them." She believed that "inquiry can't be something that is imposed." She believed that some people joined the team because of the stipend and that "some were there maybe as saboteurs."

How and why each of us maintains her unique equilibrium may help us understand why some educators resist this wisdom challenge because they may not see its relevance, why some see the relevance but proceed with caution and will resist if asked to go too far, and why some are ready for the challenge and embrace it as a way of life. The demands of this work do not necessarily require a new set of skills; insights necessary to practice this work cannot be taught or memorized. However, the consciousness that gives rise to insights can be developed by building inquiry capacity and building organizational capacity through the eight dimensions of transformative curriculum leadership (Gornik 2003; Henderson 2001). One member of the team using inquiry as a guide for discovery learned that she was "putting a wall between me and those people I was trying to support." She learned that she was not being invitational and discovered that "it was my own insecurities that made me unapproachable and perceived by others as being arrogant." Inquiry raised her consciousness and provided insights necessary to sustain the effort and meet the challenge of this reform work.

Conclusion

While much was learned throughout this two-year K–12/university collaborative, we continue to wonder how school leaders can work collaboratively with teachers to maintain an interconnectedness of high standards, sophisticated decision making, ongoing professional inquiry, and student learning while embracing transformative practices. This experience evokes many more questions than answers. If this work is so challenging, what is the prognosis for schools in societies with democratic ideals? Are there educators who want to do this work despite the cultural and political pressure? How must we organize ourselves to support the individual efforts of those who envision and enact a good educational journey for all students?

If we improve our curriculum judgment, then we will improve our schools. Under the dominant management paradigm, however, improvement is measured in terms of data-driven accountability and decision-making based on students' requisite skills, not on their abilities to live and sustain their lives. To continue this work, Henderson and Kesson (2003) argue that we must think in more expansive terms about ascertaining the quality of education and ask a different set of questions that includes the following: Does this educational decision benefit all people equally, especially those who have been marginalized in the past? What kind of "good life" does this policy envision? Does this curriculum plan add to the beauty, the richness, and the harmony of a community's life? Will this decision not just raise test scores but foster other important human characteristics as well, such as generosity, compassion, and benevolence?

Specific strategies can build personal inquiry capacity and structural organizational capacity so necessary for this transformative work. First, we must recognize that most educators are very comfortable with and fully understand the command-and-control paradigm. There exists, however, a notable portion of educators who understand and embrace *practical reasoning* while making curriculum decisions. Their openness to problem-solving curriculum decisions provides fertile ground for cultivating their inquiry capacities. The most potent force for this kind of educational change, however, rests in a smaller group of educators who use *practical wisdom* while making curriculum judgments.

Pilot programs could be put in place that provide resources and build leadership necessary for those few educators who are ready to engage in this work. Meanwhile, the district's current management paradigm would continue. Supporting this work even in small ways positions an organization to promote democratic morality and to sustain democratic educational reform.

References

Barton, J., and A. Collins. 1993. Portfolios in teacher education. *Journal of Teacher Education* 44(3): 200–210.

Burns, J. 1978. *Leadership.* New York: Harper & Row.

Costa, A., and R. Garmston. 1994. *Cognitive coaching: A foundation for renaissance schools.* Norwood, Mass.: Christopher-Gordon.

Cuban, L. 2003. *Why is it so hard to get good schools?* New York: Teachers College Press.

Darling-Hammond, L., and M. W. McLaughlin. 1995. Policies that support professional development in an era of reform. *Phi Delta Kappan* 76(8): 597–604.

Dewey, J. 1963. *Experience and education.* New York: Macmillan. (Orig. pub. 1938.)

———. 1989. *Freedom and culture.* Buffalo, N.Y.: Prometheus. (Orig. pub. 1939.)

Eisner, E. 1994. *Cognition and curriculum reconsidered.* 2nd ed. New York: Teachers College Press.

Fullan, M. 1993. *Change forces: Probing the depths of educational reform.* New York: Falmer.

Fullan, M., and A. Hargreaves. 1996. *What's worth fighting for in your school?* New York: Teachers College Press.

Gornik, R. 2003. A case study of teacher inquiry capacity. Doctoral diss., Kent State University.

Guild, P., and S. Garger. 1985. *Marching to different drummers.* Alexandria, Va.: Association for Supervision and Curriculum Development.

Guskey, T., and M. Huberman, eds. 1995. *Professional development in education: New paradigms and practices.* New York: Teachers College Press.

Hargreaves, A. 1994. *Changing teachers, changing times: Teachers' work and culture in the postmodern age.* New York: Teachers College Press.

Henderson, J. 2001. *Reflective teaching: Professional artistry through inquiry.* 3rd ed. Upper Saddle River, N.J.: Merrill/Prentice Hall.

Henderson, J., and R. Hawthorne. 2000. *Transformative curriculum leadership*. 2nd ed. Upper Saddle River, N.J.: Merrill/Prentice Hall.

Henderson, J., and K. Kesson. 2003. *Curriculum wisdom: Educational decisions in democratic societies*. Upper Saddle River, N.J.: Merrill-Prentice Hall.

Kegan, R. 1982. *The evolving self: Problem and process in human development*. Cambridge, Mass.: Harvard University Press.

———. 1994. *In over our heads: The mental demands of modern life*. Cambridge, Mass.: Harvard University Press.

Kekes, J. 1995. *Moral wisdom and good lives*. Ithaca, N.Y.: Cornell University Press.

Little, J. 1987. Teachers as colleagues. In *Educators' handbook*, edited by V. Richardson-Koehler. White Plains, N.Y.: Longman, 491–510.

Lord, B. 1994. Teachers' professional development: Critical colleagueship and the role of professional communities. In *The future of education: Perspectives on national standards in America*, edited by N. Cobb. New York: College Entrance Examination Board, 175–204.

Loughran, J., and D. Corrigan. 1995. Teaching portfolios: A strategy for developing learning and teaching in preservice education. *Teaching and Teacher Education* 11(6): 565–77.

Lyons, N., ed. 1998. *With portfolio in hand: Validating the new teacher professionalism*. New York: Teachers College Press.

Nias, J., G. Southworth, and A. Yeomans. 1989. *Staff relationships in the primary school*. London: Cassell.

Rearick, M., and A. Feldman. 1999. Orientations, purposes and reflection: A framework for understanding action research. *Teaching and Teacher Education* 15(4): 333–49.

Rosenholtz, S. 1989. *Teachers' workplace: The social organization of schools*. New York: Longman.

Sarason, S. 1990. *The predictable failure of educational reform: Can we change course before it's too late?* San Francisco: Jossey-Bass.

Schmuck, R., and P. Runkel. 1985. *The handbook of organization development in schools*. 3rd ed. Prospect Heights, Ill.: Waveland.

Schwab, J. 1978. *Science, curriculum, and liberal education: Selected essays*. Chicago: University of Chicago Press.

Sergiovanni, T. 1992. *Moral leadership: Getting to the heart of school reform*. San Francisco: Jossey-Bass.

———. 2000. *The lifeworld of leadership: Creating culture, community, and personal meaning in our schools*. San Francisco: Jossey-Bass.

Taafaki, I. 1992. Collegiality and women teachers in elementary and middle school settings: The caring relationship and nurturing interdependence. Doctoral diss., University of Massachusetts–Amherst.

Tom, A. 1984. *Teaching as a moral craft.* New York: Longman.

Walker, D. 1971. A naturalistic model for curriculum development. *School Review* 80(1): 51–65.

———. 2003. *Fundamentals of curriculum: Passion and professionalism.* 2nd ed. Mahwah, N.J.: Lawrence Erlbaum Associates.

Woods, P., ed. 1990. *Teacher skills and strategies.* New York: Falmer.

Zepeda, S. 1999. *Staff development: Practices that promote leadership in learning communities.* Larchmont, N.Y.: Eye on Education.

Exploring "Theatre as Pedagogy":   7
Silences, Stories, and Sketches of Oppression

MORNA McDERMOTT, TOWSON UNIVERSITY, TOWSON, MARYLAND
TOBY DASPIT, WESTERN MICHIGAN UNIVERSITY
KEVIN DODD, SHIFTING FORMS, KALAMAZOO, MICHIGAN

Ideally, if we were to theorize the practice of theatre as pedagogy, we would state that the "Theatre as Pedagogy" (TAP) project[1] that we collaborated on clearly demonstrates how easily theatre can be understood as pedagogy. We would proceed to explain how Paulo Freire's (1970, 1998) and Augusto Boal's (1985, 1992, 1995) visions of transformative pedagogy and theatre were clearly supported in the work conducted during our weeklong theatre project. Concrete examples from our collaborative work in the form of participant feedback would serve as "evidence" that "theatre as pedagogy" as a way to promote social justice in public schooling was "easy." We would present a "model" that shows how others can similarly use drama to change the lives of students and teachers. The data, collected from graduate students and teachers who participated in the workshop, would be so compelling to educators and school systems that they would be inspired to adopt it wholeheartedly. In this "perfect world," we could offer "drama and social transformation in three easy steps—just add water." That is not this chapter.

To echo Public Enemy's (1988) proclamation, "This time the revolution will not be televised." In other words, we are not sure what (if any) definitive conclusions we might arrive at before the credits on the back of our essay begin to roll. We hope to leave more room in this chapter for what is not known than what is. Why?

Reviewing notes collected during this summer 2001 project, we find ourselves "lost." We feel less sure of how effective our project was at actually accomplishing our aims. Yet we do feel that the various layers of intentions and outcomes did raise significant questions for others working in the fields of curriculum and theatre based on two basic premises: curriculum as a public moral enterprise is a murky "in-between" of theory and practice with no set boundaries, and the engagement between drama and pedagogy in constructing moral and socially just curricula is complex, with few if any easy answers.

In developing the schema for this chapter, we decided to foreground brief, separate monologues (to appropriate a theatrical device). The entire piece was constructed, however, as an ongoing dialogue through e-mail and face-to-face exchanges. Sometimes we disagreed; often we agreed. Beginning from similar perspectives about the need for critical transformation of teaching through engagement with drama, each of us witnessed the same series of events and experiences but from the perspectives of three different "roles" within that project. This is part of what it means to be "public"—to complicate our discord rather than to simplify it with some unified theory.

Monologue I: Kevin

A wise director with whom I worked once responded to the question "How do you want this show to affect the audience?" with "I want for them to ask the deeper questions, to be placed in dialogue with the universe." The placement of aesthetic activity in a curricular context can encourage students to do just that. James Baldwin wrote, "The purpose of art is to lay bare the questions which have been hidden by the answers" (in Bogart 2001, 82). A similar assertion was made by the philosopher Victor Schklovsky, who, in his *Four Essays on Formalism*, states, "Everything around us . . . is asleep. The function of art is to awaken what is asleep. How do you awaken what is asleep? According to Schklovsky, you turn it slightly until it awakens" (in Bogart 2001, 53).

The TAP project attempted to give the participants the opportunity to "turn" their experiences slightly and uncover the questions that lie dormant in their work as educators, specifically examining questions related to racial and ethnic issues. These participants would then be able to do the same for other teachers and students. Attempting to take the leap in the classroom and approach the "larger human issues" can be difficult, however.

"One cannot look directly at the truly big human issues any more than one can look directly at the sun," Anne Bogart (2001, 57) wrote. "In order to see the sun you look slightly to the side. Between the sun and where you are looking is your perception of the sun." The way we can shift our perceptions when approaching issues, or content, in the classroom is through metaphor. "Metaphor," to Bogart, "is that which is carried above the literalness of life. Art is metaphor and metaphor is transformation" (57). So, within an aesthetic vocabulary, metaphor is one of our primary tools. In the theatre, as with visual art and dance, we use visual metaphors. This is where Augusto Boal and the Theatre of the Oppressed enter.

Theatre as Curriculum as Democratic Discourse

Theatre or theatricality . . . allows man [*sic*] to observe himself in action, in activity. The self-knowledge . . . allows him to imagine variations of his action, to study alternatives.   —Boal 1995, 13

Theatre is an inherently public enterprise because, at its most basic level, theatre is "life's content" performed intently for the purpose of being viewed by others—the audience. Summarizing the history of theatre, Boal (1995) contends that "theatre is the first human invention" (grounded in the act of self-observation). "Observing itself, the human being perceives what it is, discovers what it is not and imagines what it could become" (116).

Theatre is not only a public enterprise but also an "aesthetic text" (Pinar et al. 1995) that reflects back and constructs human experiences to an audience through metaphoric means. Through theatre, we can "show" what is intended to be known. Bringing together the elements of public and aesthetic, theatre uses visual and metaphoric language(s) that enable us to reflect the existing human condition and, more important, to imagine what else we might become. When used as a form of social discourse, theatre leads to "the production of artifacts" that reveal existing conditions or experiences and also "functions to create anew—or reconceptualize—that situation" (Pinar et al. 1995, 593).

Many have long recognized theatre as a "central metaphor for curriculum" and even "an important sense in which curriculum *is* theatre" (Pinar et al. 1995, 589; emphasis added). In *Toward a Poor Curriculum* (Pinar and Grumet 1976), Madeleine Grumet notes the parallels between Jerzy Grotowski's work and the method of *currere* (an autobiographical method that analyzes educational experiences). Theatre, she suggests, is a way "to bring students back to a conscious sense of their own bodies, feelings, thoughts, and words" by bringing to their awareness "the specific and concrete situation within which he or she acts" (590).

This conception of curriculum, in turn, shapes how we might reenvision or reembody curriculum as well: to consider "self" as a living text that incites moral and public pedagogical discourses within the classroom. Theatre "shows" those qualities about us and our experiences that cannot be spoken. When exploring issues of race and ethnicity through theatre, we are reminded of Wilkinson's (2002) observation that "memories like corpses can be exhumed. If they come fragmented or incomplete, that is part of their story" (25).

Monologue 2: Morna

At the time I started to revisit the TAP workshop, I was also "coincidentally" reading a book about oppression and inquiry. Wilkinson's (2002) *Silence on The Mountain* details Guatemalan history over the past hundred or so years. The story begins with what was not said, what could not be asked, and the author's quest to reconstruct a narrative history from what could not be spoken. Referring to his research and interviews with oppressed workers of that region, he recalls specifically one moment "when I saw Mario tugging at that kid's hair, it occurred to me that my tugging at peoples' memories was not so different. Maybe I should leave them to their silence" (149).

Wilkinson's self-critical reflection led me to think about the roles that silence as well as language (visual and written) play in dialogue, in the reconstruction of memory, and in the history and personal experiences of oppression through drama. I thought about my concerns over leading this workshop and how my role as a white female might impact the work that would be accomplished. It reminded me of the words of postcolonial theorist Gayatri Spivak:

> I will have in an undergraduate class, let's say a young, white male student, politically-correct, who will say "I am only a bourgeois white male, I can't speak." I say to them: "Why not develop a certain degree of rage against the history that has written such an abject script for you that you are silenced?" Then you begin to investigate what it is that silences you, rather than take this very deterministic position since my skin color is this, since my sex is this, I cannot speak. (Spivak, in Ellison 1996, 370)

What "right" did I have to speak about issues of racism and oppression, to serve as the coordinator of a project where we would confront as a collective group many things that I as an individual had never experienced first-hand?

The TAP Project

The flyer advertising the TAP project notes its "official," institutional memory:

> The project seeks to develop means of incorporating race and ethnic rela-
> tions into a multicultural public school curriculum using the collaboration
> of schoolteachers, students, university researchers, administrators, and par-
> ents. Theatre will be used to facilitate dialogue among schoolteachers
> about the racial and ethnic environments in their classrooms, the obstacles
> to incorporating issues of race and ethnicity in schools, and the theatre
> strategies that can be incorporated into curricula to address unequal power
> relations, cultural histories, ideologies, and epistemologies. Participants
> will develop a "toolkit," or repertoire of theatre strategies and other rele-
> vant resources, during the intensive workshop sessions.

Reflecting on various dramatic techniques used that week and dialogue between participants, we formulated questions and concerns that challenge
the tidy promotional narrative. Instead, our concerns emerge from the
blurry gray landscape of the "in-between": the space within the seeming di-
chotomies of image and word, language and silence, and "self" and
"Other."

During this project, we emphasized techniques that highlighted the aesthetic and moral powers of theatre. According to Boal (1985), the Theatre
of the Oppressed is "a system of physical experiences, aesthetic games, image techniques and special improvisations" with the purpose of "turning
the practice of theatre into an effective tool for the comprehension of social and personal problems and the search for their solutions" (15).

If theatre as a form of public and aesthetic discourse enables us to imagine other social and moral possibilities, then perhaps the most effective way
to disempower a people is to take away their capacity and freedom to create.
To effectively colonize a people is to colonize their "sight," especially how
they see themselves in relationship to the rest of the world. Power reaffirms
itself by producing a grand narrative that tells marginalized or oppressed

groups who they are and who they can (or cannot) become. They learn to produce and to be products themselves but not to create. Similarly, theatre, as any form of human construction/communication, has the power to retell dominant narratives or, conversely, might invite a space for alternative narratives to be created or revealed.

As a form of aesthetic dialogue, the TAP project explored multiple perspectives on social justice within schooling practices, mapped together lived experiences (Daspit and McDermott 2002) of students and teachers, and used metaphors and visual/sensual languages to reveal *through* our bodies relationships between self and "Other." We were interested in the power relationships between dominant and subversive narratives told in the schools or experienced by the participants. In each of the activities, participants served as both actors and, as Boal would say, "spect-actors." We were all witnesses and narrators in exhuming the history of our shared experiences.

Addressing the challenges of constructing a democratic curriculum through theatre, project participants and we (as coordinators) struggled to construct a democratic curriculum as put forth by Henderson and Kesson (2000). We sought to examine who we defined as our "public" or audience, how we might move this "public" through theatre to address issues of oppression, and how to develop plans toward action to change oppressive elements within the educational system. This project was precisely the kind of site that bell hooks (1994) speaks of in *Teaching to Transgress*:

> Any effort to transform institutions so that they reflect a multicultural standpoint must take into consideration the fears teachers have when asked to shift their paradigms. Such a site must offer the opportunity to express those concerns while also learning to create ways to approach the multicultural classroom and curriculum. (63)

One example from the TAP project that focused on Image and Forum Theatre (Boal 1985) highlights the tensions between theory and practice, between thought and expression. We began by introducing the active theatrical vocabulary and brainstorming a list of classroom issues related to race, culture, and ethnicity. Image Theatre embraces the power of silence in discourse by showing without naming and allowing silences to speak for themselves through visual metaphor. The participants then shared, in small groups, personal narratives related to a previously brainstormed list of issues and created a group image that expressed their experience of these issues.

The participants had a difficult time allowing the images to speak for themselves. They constantly felt the need to explain their image or, at the very least, show a movement to elaborate on the image. For example, one participant, a white female in her early fifties, used her body to represent the image of racism as she witnessed it within her school, standing high on a chair turned away from the audience, hands over her eyes to blind her sight. Following her demonstration, she additionally felt compelled to "justify" her pose, which reflected the act of racism, by explaining that this was not how she perceived "Others" but how she witnessed the treatment of oppressed groups by her administration. This additional verbal explanation appeared to us to be a way for her to "distance" herself from the negative implications of oppression of the appearance of being "racist" herself.

This tendency toward language has several implications. While these images are meant to speak in a language of visual metaphors, the participants were unfamiliar with such communication. Reflecting on this struggle with the inarticulate, Bogart (2001) contends, "We label as much as we can with language in the hope that once we have named something we no longer fear it" (81). Perhaps these participants were simply cowering before the enormity of the questions posed. This was a crucial point in the process of our "training." We reached the point that seems to be the reason many educators are afraid of approaching issues of race and ethnicity directly.

Monologue 3: Toby

Sitting here mid-November on a cold Michigan night, I think about some of the ironies that have emerged during my involvement with the TAP project. Of the three of us, I clearly have the least experience with theatre, having no formal "training" or stage experience. In fact, outside seeing Boal speak a few times at the Pedagogy and Theatre of the Oppressed Annual Conference and some rather limited forays into theatre exercises in the classroom, I am very much a novice.

In thinking back on the project, I am confronted with the same issues I encounter in my university teaching and research. What are the potential hazards of theory colonizing people's experiences (Daspit 2002)? How do we move from participants being "guinea pigs" to being social activists (Higdon and Daspit 2002)? Despite viewing theatre as an aesthetic text, do institutional parameters (such as grant money) corral such experiences into the service of a technical-rationalism (Pinar et al. 1995)? And how do we not reproduce the heteronormative fantasy that is public schooling whereby male university professors instruct a feminized teaching force in "proper" methods (Pinar 1999)?

In the summer of 2002, I found myself lead coordinator of the TAP project. Morna had moved back East. Kevin was in Paris studying. We were expecting similar numbers to the previous summer. One teacher signed up.

Seen but Not Heard

The fear, I concluded, was the product of ignorance. . . . Knowing what I know now, I can see that my confidence was itself the product of ignorance— the misjudgment of a person who had never known real terror and had not yet learned how to listen to silence.   —Wilkinson 2002, 78

In considering the possibilities of using theatre as verbal and aesthetic democratic "dialogue," we wondered what spaces might be carved out for democratic "silences." Prior to beginning the week-long activity, the workshop committee considered possible ramifications of videotaping the various sessions. The five of us could not agree. Some felt that video-taping the sessions would be the only way to accurately represent and re-flect on what transpired—and to use these data as research for further discussion. Others felt that videotaping the sessions would "silence" par-ticipants from being completely honest. In accordance to Heisenberg's uncertainty principle, if we were to videotape, would that "change" what was being observed?

Finally, we agreed to allow the participants to decide. On the first day, they sat around a table to discuss the issue. There was little agreement. Some felt that videotaping would help document our process and serve as an educational resource. Others countered that it would be an invasion of the intimate nature of the work being explored. Observing this dialogue, we noticed similarities among those who wanted to be videotaped, those who were indifferent, and those who remained silent. Of most interest to us were the silences of one male and one female, both of whom were in-ternational graduate students. While feelings and opinions flowed back and forth across the table, the Chinese woman and the man from Nigeria said little unless prompted by another member to respond to a certain question.

In contrast, those who were most outspoken (either for or against the videotaping) were Caucasian and African American men and women from predominantly middle-class American communities or families. We wondered what effect the cultural differences between the outspoken and the silent might have had in their ways of interacting. We were concerned that dominant voices might override the feelings of those who did not speak loudly enough.

This dialogue session revealed a commonly held assumption that practicing democracy equals "majority rules." Such a definition of democracy parallels Boal's critique of Aristotelian catharsis, a form of theatre in which members of the theatre audience happen to be of a similar mind-set to that of the protagonist. The theatre elicits a sense of catharsis for the audience in sympathy with the plight of the "hero." Much like our Hollywood movie version, the story line and "good guys" frequently reinforce the status quo rather than challenging it.

The idea of "majority rules" as a neat and pretty version of democracy similarly "seeks [to] adapt the individual to society" and is empowering only for those who are "happy with the values of that society" (Boal 1995, 72). However, what happens when all voices are not heard? What of those voices that choose to remain silent? In what ways does this affect the roles of theatre as an instrument of change? Reflecting on the words of Wilkinson, we are left with the question: Is the ability to speak up and to include one's own voice in a democratic dialogue really an invisible privilege afforded only to those who have nothing to lose but everything to gain?

As a result of the conversation on that first day, we began thinking of democracy as a collective act in which all individuals must arrive at a consensus brought about by hearing multiple perspectives—an often "messy" and complicated process. As Boal (1995) reminds us, theatre ought to explore "multiple interrelations" and, much like the idea of democracy itself, "denote conflict, contradictions, confrontation, defiance" (16). The videotape scenario reminds us that, like democratic dialogue, theatre does not always automatically lead to empowerment.

On further critical reflection, we consider how this one particular incident also became a microcosm of the larger issues with which we were dealing. Linds (1997) asserts, "Any anti-racist education practice must examine the consequences of its work and incorporate fundamental questions about the purpose, methodology, and ideology about that process" (127). Taking the silences as potential forms of resistance, we suggested to the group that if we could not agree that videotaping would be a benefit to all, it would not take place.

As academics and activists working with theatre for social justice, we are intent on hearing what people have to say. We attempt to provide spaces where voices can be heard. However, we now rethink theatre not only as a means to promote democratic dialogue but also as a way to foreground and honor silences.

No Exits

Theatre *as* dialogue aimed toward empowerment and resistance must be emergent and unpredictable. It can go anywhere, does not follow any "script," and is empathetic–relational, from the soul rather than the mind. In essence, theatre as pedagogy produces a "both/and" discourse rather than an "either/or" dichotomy. As Linds (1997) notes, "This involves moving away from the linear duality of 'oppressor is bad; oppressed are good' and towards a dialogical performance . . . a more complex portrayal of power, with conflict between people with different identities" (133). For example, oppression is both *opaque* and *invisible* at the same time. Does public discourse in the form of theatre serve to hide or to reveal? Or, more important, what is being hidden and what revealed in theatre as pedagogy.

Like Paley's (1995) reference to Deleuze and Guattari's metaphor of the rhizome ("a virtually endless, complex, densely connected series of structures and interstructures with multiple entrances" [11]), having no unified theory is an opening for alternative discourses to inform each of our future practices. Theatre as dialogue is a rhizomatic system of language, images, and silences that evokes the power to talk *across* dominant narratives. What we might conclude with is a hope that the participants, like ourselves, will "be trying only to discover what other points of entrance" into issues of oppression "connect to" in our scholarship and teaching practices (Paley 1995, 11).

Despite the tentative, open-ended nature of our "conclusions," we remain convinced that theatre as pedagogy offers powerful and important entries into the "complicated conversation" that is curriculum (Pinar et al. 1995, 848). This conversation is enriched by consideration of the silences that we learned to "listen" to during our collaborative work—work that explores the significance of public discourses around socially progressive agendas. It is hoped that this chapter's format offers an illustration of the possibilities of dialogue, silences, and suspension of theoretical frameworks and expectations. Only when we are "emptied" of preconceived theories and answers might we become open to the transformational power of images, words, and silences within the theatre and, perhaps, realize that if there is no final answer, then the possibilities for change are also limitless.

Notes

We would like to thank the most recent members of TAP for their assistance in discussing the ideas for this chapter: Francis Bilancio, W. F. Santiago-Valles, Jin Abe, Kim Lu, Abubakar Alhassan, and Larry Mabry.

1. The Theatre as Pedagogy (TAP) project is sponsored by Western Michigan University's Lewis Walker Institute for Race and Ethnic Relations and is supported by a "Gaining Early Awareness and Readiness for Undergraduate Programs" (GEAR UP) federal grant. The project is divided into two tiers. The first was a one-week (forty hours) intensive "training" for public school teachers and graduate students (eight people representing five nationalities participated) that explored ways to improve course content and develop both teaching strategies and evaluation methods that enhance the discussion of multicultural issues through theatrical methods. The second tier was designed for both dissemination and research as participants were to conduct in-service workshops in local public schools. Of the original eight participants, four took on active roles in the project the following year, and only one in-service was conducted.

References

Boal, A. 1985. *Theatre of the oppressed.* Translated by C. McBride and M. McBride. New York: Theatre Communications Group.

———. 1992. *Games for actors and non-actors.* Translated by A. Jackson. London: Routledge.

———. 1995. *The rainbow of desire: The Boal method of theatre and therapy.* Translated by A. Jackson. London: Routledge.

Bogart, A. 2001. *A director prepares: Seven essays on art and theatre.* London: Routledge.

Daspit, T. 2002. "We will interpret us": An interview with Daniel Cavicchi. *Journal of Curriculum Theorizing* 18(2): 89–98.

Daspit, T., and M. McDermott. 2002. Frameworks of blood and bone: An alchemy of performative mapping. In *Dancing the data*, edited by C. Bagley and M. Cancienne. New York: Peter Lang, 141–56.

Ellison, J. 1996. A short history of liberal guilt. *Critical inquiry* 22(2): 344–71.

Freire, P. 1970. *Pedagogy of the oppressed*. New York: Herder and Herder.

——. 1998. *Pedagogy of freedom: Ethics, democracy and civic courage*. Lanham, Md.: Rowman & Littlefield.

Henderson, J., and K. Kesson. 2000. Curriculum work as public intellectual leadership. In *Democratic curriculum theory and practice: Retrieving public spaces*, edited by K. Sloan and J. Sears. Troy, N.Y.: Educators International Press, 1–23.

Higdon, S., and T. Daspit. 2002. From guinea pigs to activists: Social transformation through oral histories and academic service learning. Paper presented to the Third Annual Curriculum and Pedagogy Conference, Decatur, Georgia, October.

hooks, b. 1994. *Teaching to transgress: Education as the practice of freedom*. New York: Routledge.

Linds, W. 1997. Burrowing below ground or just scratching the surface: A critique of Theatre of the Oppressed as anti-racist praxis. *Journal of Critical Pedagogy* 1(2). www.wmc.edu/academics/library/pub/jcp/issue1-2/linds.html (accessed May 30, 2003).

Paley, N. 1995. *Finding art's place: Experiments in contemporary education and culture*. New York: Routledge.

Pinar, W. 1999. Response: Gracious submission. *Educational Researcher* 28(1): 14–15.

Pinar, W., and M. Grumet. 1976. *Toward a poor curriculum*. Dubuque, Iowa: Kendall/Hunt.

Pinar, W., W. Reynolds, P. Slattery, and P. Taubman. 1995. *Understanding curriculum: An introduction to the study of historical and contemporary curriculum discourses*. New York: Peter Lang.

Public Enemy. 1988. *It takes a nation of millions to hold us back*. New York: Def Jam Recordings.

Wilkinson, D. 2002. *Silence on the mountain: Stories of terror, betrayal, and forgetting in Guatemala*. New York: Houghton Mifflin.

Taking Teachers to the Street   8

SUSAN FINLEY, WASHINGTON STATE UNIVERSITY, VANCOUVER
JASON ADAMS, WASHINGTON STATE UNIVERSITY, VANCOUVER

In this chapter, we trace some of the multiple iterations and connections between theories and practices that each of us, Susan and Jason, put to use as inquirers—as learners—and as teachers. Specifically, we draw theory from three dimensions of our shared experiences. We describe our relationship as student and professor, we analyze aspects of our practices of art in community, and we share reflections about our classroom-centered teaching practices. Our intention is to explore these experiences for their usefulness in understanding and theorizing about teaching and learning. Thus, we include narratives constructed from our journals and from dialogues with each other. In our dialogues, we explore connections between theory and practice in our shared experience as teacher educator and student. We conclude with discussion of how theory, informed by practice, forms a space for Jason to shape his teaching.[1]

Susan and Jason: Developing a Collaborative Working Relationship Based on Mutual Respect and Caring

What is the interplay between life experience and theory? What is the purpose of theory building, and how do we do it? We tell life stories in order to construct theories for continued living, and our descriptive narratives are often the source of our making meanings about ourselves and our worlds. As Freire (1998) says, we learn to "read the world." Yet Strauss (1995) has argued that although narrative descriptions are necessary for creating, challenging, and reporting general theories, narrative descriptions of personal events and interpretive dialogues are of limited use in theory building. That is, narratives and dialogues must first be informed and shaped by ongoing social, political, and cultural narratives of many and diverse types. Multiple but linked descriptions (along with multiple perspectives on events) are then taken together with bits and pieces of previous theory—all of which are connected and subjected to imaginative reinterpretation. This interplay of multiple strands of meaning making across time and through multiple venues etches a composite theory for understanding life into descriptive narratives. That is how practice drives theory—and it also depicts the complicated paths by which theory leaves its traces in day-to-day practice. Thus, these narrative descriptions of our student–teacher relationship and our narratives about homelessness and street life are part of the intertext that we call "theory."

> *Jason:* I believe Susan's and my collaborative relationship flowed naturally from our caring for one another as we developed a friendship beyond our professor/student relationship. There was a lot of trust in the building of our friendship. I found myself opening up to Susan about my life experiences, including having been homeless, living on the streets and in squats. But what I could share with her, I could not as easily share with others in my teacher education student cohort. It can be hard to connect sometimes when people in the class are speculating as to what hard times must be like, while you're thinking, "Wow. I slept under a porch in a cardboard box." I found it difficult during preservice teaching instruction not to talk about my experiences of homelessness, but I also felt that it was absolutely necessary to say as little as possible. No matter how open people are and how much they try not to judge someone on one's past, inevitably there are some societal engrams that rear their ugly heads.
>
> Additionally, I want to really try to keep myself in present time emotionally. I am able to look at much of my experience subjectively, but there is pain there. I know I am not in that space anymore, and I keep peace in my soul and am very aware of creating the safest environment I can for the learners I work with. I just feel so guarded because I feel like being in this teacher education program is such a great opportunity to really be in an occupation that I enjoy.
>
> Working with Susan came about by making a personal connection because of my street experiences, not despite them. We would get together and share stories of life on the streets. And we would talk endlessly about street artists that we have known, and we would share some of our artwork

with each other, poetry and paintings, and my music. Thus, by sharing our mutual interests in street life and art life, Susan and I began to understand each other. For example, the ideas and experiences about making art that we shared with each other stemmed from what was natural to each of us: we both enjoy doing art, and we each work through issues and dilemmas in our lives through art making.

Our friendship was born out of shared values. Both of us attach importance to experiences we had in street life, and we each value expressions of life that take form in street arts. For instance, we believe that alternative experiences like street life can provide unique and important perspectives on issues and theories in education. As "world citizens," we believe in the human spirit's fight for survival through self-expression. As Susan's student, I was able to express my interests in street art because she was receptive and inspirational about the subject. When I articulated how much I valued the diversity of experiences expressed among homeless youth through their art, Susan encouraged me to work with homeless youths and children. She believed that by working with youths whose experiences were similar to mine, I would be situated to reflectively understand my experiences of street life and the creative activities I engaged in while living on the street—and that I would begin to find ways to bring those experiences into my teaching.

Having been homeless, I have glimpses into society's cracks. I know its failures at instilling hope in all its children. I spent a considerable amount of time living on the streets and in squats; I didn't see a way out. My education certainly didn't prepare me to live on the streets, it didn't even prepare me to live life. I never seemed to live up to other people's expectations. If you can look to education as an act of becoming, then there is no end product of education, no perfection "by the book."

Having fallen through the cracks, I know how on edge kids are and what potential there is for them slipping through to the other side. The daily toil of staying alive sharpens the senses, brings intuition and awareness to learning. Being homeless gives you a constant sense of knowing that wherever you go, you're changing and adapting. When you're homeless, you don't have expectations of things going just one way. You allow situations to develop and then make adjustments. You just enjoy the way they are going, accepting difference, surprise, and disorder.

My most recent experience of homelessness began in summer term. Going back to school included the choice of being homeless. I could not afford to go to school and have housing. Because I spent most nights sleeping in my band's practice space, I saw it as more of a nomadic existence than as homeless in the ways I had previously experienced. I also had access to several apartments or basements, whether it be friends who were out of town or couch surfing.

During that summer I discovered that the more I would write about my homeless experience, the more it would unfold. Like an onion, I peeled back layers upon layers about the things I had done or had been done to me. Looking back at my journals that I had written when I was street homeless, I realized that my feelings, hopes, and fears about homelessness were captured in my art. Writing was my way of trying to stay connected with the other side.

In the beginning of our relationship, we based our thinking about our collaboration on interpretations of similar personal events. From there we enriched our discussion with discourse about shared experiences in the teacher education classroom. Once we had described it, we could theorize about the meaning behind the shared experience. Susan shared with Jason her thinking about how he might use his experiences to enhance his teaching practices. As he wrote about his homeless experiences, she narrated her experiences of her relationship with Jason, bringing theories about teaching and learning and curriculum into their conversations.

Susan: My concepts of caring are rooted in Nell Noddings's (1992) discourse about the responsibility of educators to provide a curriculum in which care is recognized as a fundamental, moral undertaking of schools. For Noddings, you have to care "about" someone in order to care "for" that person. Further, she insists that caring has to be reciprocal—that both persons in a relationship have to care about and for each other. Jason understood this intuitively. He described our relationship as that of being equals and of being friends who care about one another.

My notion of a curriculum of care included finding ways to involve students in a caring way with each other in multiple educational communities and to include care for society and social justice within the realm of caring community. Usually I provide opportunities for students to work in field experiences with homeless children, youths, and their families. In particular, I encouraged Jason to work in direct service with street kids. Like many street youth, Jason had kept journals of his travels and experiences, which included diaries, short stories, and poems. He is a musician who performs regularly with a local group in pubs and other venues, and he paints, now that he has a space in which to live and work. It seemed reasonable in this context, therefore, that I encourage Jason to draw on his extensive experiences for his field experience projects. Having been involved in several ongoing inquiry projects that involved street youth in various arts and writing experiences (such as Finley 2000), I suggested that Jason marry his arts-based street experiences with an educational project for homeless street youth.

Homelessness is an alienating condition that meets with zero tolerance, "not in my back yard" policies, and "invisibility" or "otherness" (National Coalition for the Homeless 2002, 2003). Jason has been fully aware that these attitudes could follow him into the higher-education classroom and even into the workplace after graduation. Meanwhile, the effects of the homeless experience were bound to be important to his self-image, so it was evident to me that our teaching and learning relationship would need to be a space in which Jason would be able to embrace ambiguities he felt about his homelessness. I wanted to provide educational opportunities for critical distance to develop for Jason to reflect on his homeless experiences and to realize that he could use his unique experiences as the basis for teaching and learning. Although his reasons for not being completely forthcoming about his life experiences were sound, I was concerned that he be able to accept himself and his life history. Maxine Greene (1988) poignantly describes the loss of freedom inured through self-denial where we find "the sketch that is our life a sketch for nothing, an outline with no picture" (9). I wanted to find ways for Jason to be authentic while also protecting his future interests. To me, this was an instance in which self-reflection about teaching practice would help authenticate Jason's experiences.

People need to learn to read their lived worlds, and responsible educators must construct social conditions that can empower people to act and grow. I asked Jason to picture his life for me in narratives—and, because ours is a caring relationship and we each have stories to tell about our experiences of street life, we began to draw a picture that included both of us.

Importantly, Jason had already claimed what Greene (1988, 22) might call "authorship" of his world. He grasped the possibility of new experience and of shaping his future by not passively accepting the social structures of homelessness, even as he was ensconced in them. Eagerly, he took up the tasks of teaching and learning in an inquiry about homelessness that included his self-reflections.

Working within the context of these layered narratives, how were we to develop a theory of teaching and learning that values personal experiences that take place outside schools? How to impart the value of experiences that are typified as negative social events such as homelessness and performing street art for money? From our shared narratives and within the contextual constraints of communications between two people, how could we thoughtfully respond to our developing notions of the impact of care on students' learning? Finally, how does each of us, Jason and Susan, utilize those theories as we continue teaching?

Practicing Art in Community

Susan designed and coordinates the Homeless and Poverty Project at Washington State University, Vancouver (WSUV). The project involves about twenty teachers and preservice teachers in educational enrichment programs for in-school children, aged six to twelve years, who reside in a homeless shelter and a neighboring transitional housing complex. At the shelter program, teaching interns from WSUV have designed and taught project-based learning through a summer camp, a one-week sports camp, music appreciation Fridays, and a series of field trips that include visits to the university as a way to establish early expectations among homeless children that college is an option. From various perspectives and approaches, teacher–participants then apply their learning about homelessness and poverty in their classrooms.

Jason was one of those students. He worked with a group of local artists who provide arts education to street kids in a studio environment. In the context of that setting, he honed his skills at painting and teaching. Eventually, he saw an opportunity to work more closely with others in his cohort by bringing his skills as an artist and his techniques for teaching art to their learning environment.

With Jason and other participating teachers, the ten children who were attending the educational enrichment program in poverty housing (a shelter and transitional housing complex) designed and painted a mural (consisting of four sixteen-square-foot panels) about their life experiences. The mural is portable in order to be used as a teaching tool in multiple settings. These children also wrote or dictated their narrative accounts of creating the mural and of the meanings they took from it.

Jason: In preparing for the mural project with children at [the shelter], Susan and I discussed details that would turn the artistic experience into a positive and memorable one for these homeless youth. I felt as though the background Susan had given me for understanding inquiry-based learning was allowing me to really feel comfortable about making shifts and changes in the planning of the painting. Susan had been very supportive in all aspects of the project, collaborating in every detail along the way. For example, Susan ordered the canvases, and I picked them up and stored them at my place until the prep work was to be done on them. Susan made me feel as though I was a legitimate researcher, even though this was my first true research project. Her confidence in me made me feel at ease with the project. It had an enormous impact on the success of the whole experience for all of us.

We met and decided that the project should be videotaped. In filming the event, something quite unexpected and wonderful happened. Some of the homeless youths began taking turns using the video camera and filming the activities of each other painting. I could tell that this was really making them feel as if they owned the project from all angles. They had ownership in the brainstorming of the project, they had ownership in the creation of the project, and now they had ownership in the documenting of the project. Susan was a great collaborator because she had experience with research and knew how to draw the children out, modeling ways to reach these homeless youth. The children really felt like we were there for them and that it was their day; these were their murals. I felt that we worked well together as a team because we were not only collaborating on the project as student and professor but as friends sharing a common interest—that is, allowing homeless children to feel valued and successful in their creativity.

As Jason's arts-education projects mutated through various forms and formats, they drew conceptually from Susan's ongoing inquiry that uses the arts to understand the aesthetic experiences of street youths and children living in shelters.

Susan: My theoretical framework for arts-based instruction with homeless and extremely poor children is rooted in those critical and feminist educators and artists who recognize creative expression as the conceptual source for personal emancipation (such as Greene 1995; hooks 1994; Morgen 1983).

In designing the murals project, Jason and I worked from our various experiences of street life, which suggested that involvement in creative expression could be one means of moving children into unfamiliar and liberated spaces in their educational lives. Despite the preparatory work that was done for the mural painting (for example, conversations with the children about what they might want to represent and even some drawings of crayon and charcoal on paper to plan some of the images that would be represented on the murals), all preconceptualization just fell by the wayside on the actual day of painting. We let that happen. When the children began applying color to these huge canvases, they were delighted with the size of the backgrounds, the variety of colors, the techniques for spreading paint, and even their feelings from brushing paint onto welcoming surfaces. It was all very visceral. We went with the moment, encouraging the children to enjoy a spontaneous art of the present rather than reproduction of the past.

Painting the murals was not an opportunity for refinement of the children's drawing techniques. Rather, it became an opportunity for the children to follow the flow of their intuitive responses to a creative process. It became clear to us that representing oneself cannot be learned analytically or outside of the moment of the experience. At one time Jason and I had wanted to display the murals in a kind of traveling show to encourage viewers to take an interest in these kids and the plight of homelessness. Standing back, I think such a display would misrepresent what the children experienced. Artists and art teachers have since agreed that the finished murals, when viewed as objects of art, lack basic and expected qualities of method and, as such, would probably provoke more comment about the children's lack of artistic skill than interest in what the children spoke about themselves through their creative experience. Lost in that would be attention to the incredible process that took place in creating the painted canvases. In our construction, we allowed learning to emerge, and we valued process over product.

From Street to Classroom:
(E)merging Theory and Classroom Practice

Very generally, the mural painting experience seemed to be quite successful in terms of students' empowerment. What several of the students had liked most about the experience was the freedom to say and paint whatever they wanted. Some of the older children (twelve to fourteen years) mentioned how much they had enjoyed working together on the canvases. A more in-depth analysis of the children's experience will have to wait for another time. Here our purpose is to discuss how we constructed theory about teaching and learning from our experiences of teaching and learning.

Jason: Since the shelter project, I have used more arts-based lessons in my classroom (grade 4). I have begun to give the students at least one chance each day to draw while listening to music or some other sort of open-ended artistic activity. From the experience of working with the children, I was able to recognize the ability of all children to "own" their education and to create their learning experiences. Recently, I modeled an assignment called "moving pictures." The assignment consisted of folding paper to create segments for Popsicle stick people to be inserted and then to narrate the events of students' spring break. I noticed that students were frequently emotional in their narrations. Each student analyzed and reflected on the mood and actions that took place in their lives, using color, drawings, dialogue, and performance.

I've been thinking about other ways of bringing the shelter [mural painting] experience back into my classroom. I'm also considering the interrelations of education in what seems to be an antieducational society. With bonds failing because school districts can't "sell" the importance of funding education to the public, how do we supply students with basic needs in order to allow them to have the tools to learn?

In homeless children's lives we see that their families have gone through periods of poor circumstances compounded by desperate decision making. I think we have to reexamine our values in schools and retool the entire approach with which we look at success. "Humanity will not survive without more advanced forms of social organization, ones capable of surpassing this articulated chaos of corporate interests that we have come to call neoliberalism, and that manages technology of irreversible, universal impact" (Dowbor 2000, 2).

Working with homeless youth, I found myself asking, "How much will a project/experience like this mural project make a child want to come back to art in an expressive manner?" "What are they getting out of it?" In asking these questions about my classroom, I will be a better teacher and learner. When we do an open-ended art lesson, I will allow the children to follow their instincts and let them play in order to learn.

Susan taught me how to allow art to happen for all those involved. There were different children working at different paces, and she was encouraging them that their pace was acceptable and their contribution to the painting was valuable. That was validation for them as *artists*. I was aware of the children's excitement to paint. I was conscious of it in their body language, voice levels, and energy bursts. As Freire (2000) wrote, "Consciousness about the world, which implies consciousness about my-self in the world, with it and with others, which also implies our ability to realize the world, to understand it, is not limited to a rationalistic experi-ence" (94). These children were experiencing art *and* experiencing them-selves for themselves, knowing there were no grades to be given; they were learning for themselves.

At the opening of this chapter, Jason described learning as "an act of becoming." He situated himself empathetically to link memories of his life with the current experiences of homeless children. From that stance, he speculated that educational equity can be achieved when process is valued over products and when diverse learning experiences are valued, including those experiences in which intuition, awareness, and the ability to adapt to new situations are valuable traits in learners. In the second excerpt, Jason had begun to identify himself as an educator and a collaborator in the ed-ucation of the children. On the basis of his experiences, he also began to put into practice some of what he had theorized about learning. He al-lowed the children to take over the camera and follow their own intuitive approaches, even where that meant abandoning carefully planned and ra-tionally defined activities. Jason relied on what he had learned in the street in much the same way that the children did, allowing intuition and adapt-ability to guide his teaching. In the final transcription, Jason ventured into the construction and expansion of theory. Working from the background of multiple narrative descriptions that the children provided about their lives, he analyzed those experiences from the vantage points of his home-less experience and from the educational theorists he is reading as part of his work with Susan. The connection of these various points of view, con-comitant with his confident use of imaginative "play," encouraged Jason to construct new lessons and approaches to teaching and learning in his class-room.

Through the enactment of teaching and learning practices grounded in a theory of care, we have used our layered narratives to construct theories of teaching and learning that value the experiences of homelessness and poverty and that pull those experiences into our constructions of caring educational communities. We are finding new ways to bring care for individuals and their personal experiences into our teaching.

Note

1. In writing up our experiences in the way we have done, it is a danger that we might lead a reader to presume that theory was used in a process of diagnostics and prescribed responses; rather, our curriculum work emerged in this instance by virtue of circumstances and predilection to certain forms of action—although our actions bear the traces of theory. As a result, our discourse about curricular practices enacted in these examples is grounded in and informed by the events that emerged in practice.

References

Dowbor, L. 2000. Foreword. In *Pedagogy of the heart*, by P. Freire. New York: Continuum, 21–28.

Finley, S. 2000. "Dream child": An approach to creating poetic dialogue in homeless research. *Qualitative Inquiry* 6(3): 432–34.

Freire, P. 1998. *Pedagogy of the oppressed*. New York: Continuum.

———. 2000. *Pedagogy of the heart*. New York: Continuum.

Greene, M. 1988. *The dialectic of freedom*. New York: Teachers College Press.

———. 1995. *Releasing the imagination*. San Francisco: Jossey-Bass.

hooks, b. 1994. *Teaching to transgress: Education as the practice of freedom*. New York: Routledge.

National Coalition for the Homeless. 2002. *Illegal to be homeless: The criminalization of homelessness in the United States*. www.nationalhomeless.org/crimreport/index.html (accessed May 24, 2003).

———. 2003. *Hate crimes and violence against people experiencing homelessness*. www.nationalhomeless.org/hatecrimes/annual.html (accessed May 24, 2003).

Noddings, N. 1992. *The challenge to care in schools: An alternative approach to education*. New York: Teachers College Press.

Morgen, S. 1983. Toward a politics of "feelings": Beyond the dialectic of thought and action. *Women's Studies* 10: 203–23.

Strauss, A. 1995. Notes on the nature and development of general theories. *Qualitative Inquiry* 1(1): 7–18.

It Is Not Resolved Yet: When a Louisiana French Immersion Activist Engages Postcolonial, Feminist Theory (or Vice Versa)

9

NINA ASHER, LOUISIANA STATE UNIVERSITY
MICHELLE HAJ-BROUSSARD, LAFAYETTE PARISH SCHOOL
   DISTRICT, LAFAYETTE, LOUISIANA

This chapter is a dialogue between a "theorist" who draws on postcolonial and feminist theory in education and a "practitioner" who teaches in a Louisiana French immersion elementary school in a heritage language context.[1] Our dialogue began when Michelle enrolled in an "Identity, Culture, Curriculum" (ICC) seminar offered by Nina. Focused on the education of those "on the margins," each of us interrogates the intersecting forces of race, culture, and class in particular social and geographic contexts through theory, research, and practice.

Over the past ten years, I (Michelle) have been teaching students from low-income families in elementary French immersion schools in Acadiana, where French is a heritage language. As an activist, I have served as the secretary for the Louisiana Consortium of Immersion Schools and the president of *Action cadienne*, a nonprofit group promoting French in Louisiana. My doctoral dissertation examines the experiences of African American students in the French immersion context.

I (Nina) am an assistant professor in the Department of Curriculum and Instruction at Louisiana State University, Baton Rouge. The three distinct yet intersecting areas in which I write and teach are postcolonial and feminist theory, multiculturalism, and Asian American education. I am a South Asian woman, born in "postcolonial" India. I did my graduate work in New York City and now teach in the Deep South. My theory and practice are informed by a self-reflexive interrogation of the dynamic, context-specific intersections of race, culture, class, gender, and geographic location (Asher 2001, 2003).

In this chapter, we unpack the tensions emerging from the recursive "dialogue" between theory and practice not only between the two of us but also in terms of each of us maintaining integrity between her own theory and practice. Each of us discusses, in the first person, how her particular, self-reflexive engagement with postcolonial, feminist theory has been both productive and unsettling. The dialogue develops as we respond to and build on each other's reflections. Conscious of the colonization implied in hierarchical splits between "theory" and "practice," "teacher" and "student," we note that each responded candidly and thoughtfully to the other's input to enhance the integrity and clarity of our individual voices and this chapter.

Reflections on Theory in Relation to Practice

In this section, we dialogue about our respective struggles and epiphanies in bringing theory and practice together. Each of us discusses how she navigated troubling contradictions in the process.

Michelle's Reflections

bell hooks (1994) suggests that theory heals. However, as I engaged the theoretical perspectives I encountered in Nina's ICC class, I felt wounded. Theory shook me out of my complacent belief that I was doing "right" by working with marginalized students. Theory made me sharply conscious of the diseases of racism and prejudice afflicting schools and society. Further, I encountered the "tangles of implication" (Britzman 1997) when I recognized myself as a participant in the oppressive structures and practices I was trying to change. I realized that addressing marginalization is a complex, contradictory process in which I was both "colonizer/colonized" (Villenas 1996). Theory healed me like salt—there was shock and pain, and times when I wished I could continue believing that these wounds were not too bad and could just let them be. As my recursive reflections here illustrate, the tension between theory and practice is not resolved.

THEORY AND ME: MY TEACHING PRACTICE I am an "outsider" in the context in which I teach—I am a white teacher, with little francophone heritage, in a francophone heritage school, with majority African American students. My question, then, is, Why do I choose to work as an "outsider"?

Teaching in a francophone region, I became aware of the hostile climate that marginalizes French as an unwanted, "foreign" language. For instance, one principal expressly forbade French teachers to speak French in her presence. Heritage French speakers narrated stories of being forced to kneel on rice for not speaking English at school. While I immediately saw how francophones were marginalized, it took me longer to understand how African American students were also "othered." As my engagement with theory deepened, I recognized my own unexamined complicity in the "othering" of African American students and my own blindness to racial oppression. I saw white teachers "denying the salience of race" (Sleeter 1993, 161). I used to maintain that my students' race did not influence my teaching, but I realized that this was false. I experienced pangs of guilt on noticing, for example, that I penalized mostly African American boys. From then on, I taught with trepidation, questioning myself at every step. My dis-ease emerged from my new consciousness of racism and prejudice, which displaced me from my comfort zone, leading me to interrogate my own practice, my own *implicatedness*.

THEORY AND ME: MY COLLEAGUES Armed only with a B.A. in French, I fell into teaching with no experience or credentials. While I am somewhat of an outsider to the teaching community, I experienced a sense of camaraderie with my colleagues. They were helpful, caring, and generous: sharing tips for handling the workload, celebrating marriages and birthdays, and supporting one another through difficult times.

However, applying theory to practice, I gained different perspectives on the teaching collectivity. Feeling like the "outsider within" (Collins 1991), I saw how camaraderie also encompassed hostile perspectives toward students, parents, and racial minority teachers. For instance, my colleagues referred to a housing project where a number of "problem" students lived as "Crazy Fields" instead of "Country Fields." Such negative comments were hushed whenever parents or minority teachers entered the room. hooks (1990) suggests "choosing the margin" as a "site of resistance" (153). My new awareness fed my activism. I began speaking up in the teachers' lounge, questioning our collective practices and our prejudiced beliefs about parents and students. When a colleague spoke of African American students' vernacular as "bad English," I disagreed, arguing that language is an important part of identity, culture, and context.

At the same time, I question how effective I can be, as the "outsider within," in transforming the teaching community. As an insider, I know that ranks close in when the teaching collectivity feels under attack. Yet my consciousness as an outsider impels me to speak up against our own prejudices.

Nina's Reflections

For me, theory and practice have always been intertwined. My engagement with theory emerged and has grown from my practice. For instance, in the mid-1980s, I worked with "underprivileged" high school students from the "Scheduled Tribes" in India.[2] I found myself questioning the alienating English curriculum to which these students were subjected, particularly since they lived in rural areas, came from non-English-speaking families, and, indeed, were the first generation to attend school. I was appalled that the educational system was so oppressive—colonized *and* colonizing—and that it required students to pass state board English examinations in order to enter college. Inspired by Freire (1998), I began to consider the importance of contextually relevant curriculum and pedagogy and the implications for decolonizing education.

My geographic shifts and the apparent contradictions resulting from them have also informed my engagement with theory. A South Asian scholar in the United States, as "academic Self," I am at home in the academy, and, simultaneously, as "woman of color Other," I am the outsider (Asher 2001). As a "[post]colonial hybrid," my use of English to deconstruct colonial discourse is a necessary irony, as the alternative is to remain "silent, in-scribed" (Asher 2002, 87). The recent move from New York City to Louisiana further informs and troubles my pedagogical practice in the multicultural teacher education classroom. I have debated how postcolonial feminism intersects with the experience of living in the Deep South in productive ways (Asher 2003). Thus, acknowledging my *implicatedness* enables and informs my efforts toward transformation.

This praxis of critical, self-reflexive interrogation allows me to maintain openness and integrity between theory and practice. For instance, students in my undergraduate multicultural education classes are mostly young white women from Louisiana with varying degrees of trepidation about multiculturalism. Indeed, they see themselves and their lives as unrelated to this issue. However, through a self-reflexive, dialogical process, students begin "discovering" that despite their apparent homogeneity, they do represent differences. Often students find themselves interrogating attitudes toward race across generations, within their families; their own interracial encounters and struggles; and stories of peers with Jewish ancestry or gay children. Thus, such apparently abstract concepts as "in-betweenness" and "fluidity of culture" gain meaning for my students.

The Inner Dialogue:
Working the Tensions between Theory and Practice
In this section, each of us grapples with how integrating theory and practice results in shifts in perspectives. Each of us finds, once again, that there are new struggles and new possibilities.

Michelle's Inner Dialogue
Like Anzaldúa's (1987) mestiza, I want to be on "both shores at once" (78). As a practitioner, I want to stay within the teaching collectivity. My teaching "keeps it real," requiring me to negotiate my relations with students, colleagues, and theory on a daily basis. As a theorist, I want to feed my activism and reflect critically on my practice. However, I find that theory distances me from the teaching collectivity. As a practitioner, I know that teachers are scrutinized under the microscope of educational research. At the same time, my own engagement with research and theory has revealed to me how, through self-reflexive praxis, teachers can address oppression to transform educational practice. Sustained change comes from within, and empowerment emerges from a *conscientização* of one's own situation (Freire 1998). Thus, straddling the border between theory and practice and working recursively with the dynamic tensions at that juncture, I combine my sense of responsibility toward my students and colleagues with a sense of agency, sustaining my activism and maintaining integrity as I teach marginalized students.

Yet as a practitioner and a newcomer to theory, I expected critical theory and educational research to help me "fix" the context and practice of teaching. Disappointingly, my new insights did not improve my teaching context in radical ways. During ICC, Nina read a poem about the recursive process of research and conscientization in which the poet talked about how journeying through "lost-ness" can bring one close to death and how "death sensed is source again" (Mooney 1975, 173). Lost *is* how I felt when the theories from class bombarded my head while I was teaching. As I began giving up my safe place, my teaching nook, to "come out" as a theorist, I rethought my initial response to Pratt's (1984) story of coming out as a lesbian. Although I realize that the two experiences are vastly different, each of us relinquished our comfort zone and place of safety to move toward transformation.

I began turning my analytical gaze onto myself and my colleagues, seeing the disease of racism and prejudice, and experiencing dis-ease within my classroom and the teaching collectivity. However, while reflexivity requires that I consider what I am doing, teaching requires me to be in the moment. How can I do both at once? In discussing issues of self-reflexivity and integrity as a researcher and educator in class, Nina acknowledged that "cutting edge" research can leave behind particles, "sawdust," to fall unheeded to the ground (Asher 2001). My constant struggle to negotiate between my distancing theoretical perspective and the close, emotional engagement necessary to interact with students led to my biggest unresolved dilemma: in what ways are the students becoming the sawdust? Perhaps my discomfort emerged from breaking down borders between practitioner and theorist and "learning through conflict" (Kumashiro 2000) in this process.

As a "white"[3] teacher/researcher, who teaches mostly African American students, I am constantly "complicating the relations of power" (Britzman 1997, 32). I have learned that my students are more adept than I am at seeing inequality—*they* are the experts at sensing oppression. They *know* which teachers are cruel, that they are still segregated, and that being bused across town is part of the price they will have to pay for "desegregation." In light of their critical observations of such serious social injustices, school rules, such as maintaining silence when the teacher speaks or walking on the blue line, seem not just authoritarian but petty and trivial as well. At the same time, I waver between empathizing with my fellow teachers and seeing their attitudes toward and treatment of our students as oppressive. Thus, I find that my own process of *conscientização* has thrown my teaching askew. I am compelled to question how and why I create relationships with my students and colleagues. What does theory offer me in recompense for these sacrifices?

Critical theory does not offer teachers a "solution"; it is not a *recette toute faite*. There are no cutesy activities and fun songs with the promise of improved results. Rather, theory offers a chance to step outside and go beyond passive participation in a diseased system. Theory is like the little red pill that Morpheus offers Neo in the popular film *The Matrix*. If Neo takes the red pill, he gets to see "how far the rabbit hole goes." "All I'm offering is the truth," Morpheus says. When Neo realizes that he cannot go back, Morpheus asks, "But if you could, would you really want to?" (Wachowski and Wachowski 1999). My answer, like Neo's, is "No." Theory is not a set path one follows; it is more like a key that opens a prison door. What I do now is my own construction. I make my own path.

Nina's Inner Dialogue

Wow! I find Michelle's candid self-awareness exhilarating. The exhilaration comes from the "aha!-ness" of dialogue between theory and practice and the rigorous, recursive process that unsettles complacency, opens doors, and helps heal the wounds of racism, sexism, homophobia, classism, and colonization. At the same time, there is the exhaustion that comes from seeing oneself as the mouse at the foot of the mountain of oppression—a mouse nested within this terrain. I can either nest passively in this terrain or work to deconstruct, rethink, and transform. Yes, Michelle, like you, compelled to seek answers, I enrolled in a doctoral program nearly twenty years ago. I swallowed that red pill sans turning back.

Of course, my particular recursive process takes a different twist. Having turned to theory after experiencing the disease of injustice within the education system, today my practice is comprised of teaching theory and research. My challenge is not getting too complacent in the comfort zone of theory and (shudder!) teaching it as infallible; *that* would be the kind of lost-ness that leads to death. So, perhaps the question is not so much whether one is a "theorist" or "practitioner" but rather how, as either/both, one does not get smug, complacent, and close-minded. For me, one way to "keep it real" is to listen to my students, engage their context-specific lived experiences, and invite their interpretations of theory. For instance, as I taught ICC, students struggled with reading Bhabha's (1994) *Location of Culture*. In fact, some were upset, maybe even angered, that they were required to deal with such dense text. Although I found this response unsettling, I was aware that fear often underlies angry resistance. Besides, I reminded myself that theory is suspect for many students in education, even at the graduate level—a troubling reflection of the larger culture of deintellectualizing teaching. As the teacher, I worked self-reflexively to incorporate this tension rather than simply explaining it away as inevitable resistance to theory. Bearing in mind that beginning with where the students are is critical to good teaching, I continued to invite students to reflect on their agreements and disagreements with the readings, in class discussions and via written "reading logs." I believe that only by working through their own fear/resistance would the students be able to engage the theories in any meaningful way.

As the course progressed, some of the resistance began metamorphosing into attitudes of openness to "new," critical ideas. Michelle was among those who found herself going back to Bhabha's writing and sharing, with great excitement, the interpretations and analyses that were unfolding for her. For me, such a pedagogical process, which requires grappling with differences, although not necessarily easy, is critical because it allows both student and teacher to engage theory in productive ways. Even now, engaging Michelle's struggles as a mestiza (Anzaldúa 1987) on the shores of practice and theory reminds me to continue doing the same to maintain the rigor and relevance of my own work. Indeed, I believe that each of us would lose out if either sought an easy reconciliation or a clear-cut diametrical disagreement between (her) theory and (her) practice. It is the self-reflexive, often troubling, and unsettling process of working through the tensions that is ultimately transformative.

As Anzaldúa (1987) has argued, it is the ongoing process of negotiating differences across contexts and cultures that allows for developing a consciousness of the borderlands, see oneself as mestiza, and get past such binaries as West and East, oppressor and oppressed, Northeast and Deep South, theorist and practitioner. Perhaps, then, my most productive identification is "theorist/practitioner" and my most productive work in theory and research is informed by my engagement with contextual and cultural differences encountered in the realm of practice.

After the Red Pill: Recursion

In concluding, Michelle and Nina discuss, in turn, the recursive, self-reflexive process that allows each of them to maintain integrity within and across the realms of practice and theory, theory and practice.

Teaching, Theory, and Michelle's Re-Visioning of the Self

When I began my dialogue with Nina, I was reluctant to call myself a theorist. I believed that theorists lived in ivory towers, apart from "real" educators who were responsible for young students, interacted with parents, and dealt with the daily administrative grind. I now see theory as integral to my teaching. I see how easy it is for overworked teachers to fall back on cultural deficiency models to explain students' failures or resistance instead of critically interrogating larger issues of race, class, and so on. Indeed, when my African American boys laugh at my punishments, I wonder how my own actions and responses in the classroom may feed their resistance. Theory opens a critical, self-reflexive process and allows me to go beyond such convenient binaries as "good" and "bad" parents/students, "right" and "wrong" teaching methods. Life is messier with theory; the boundaries begin to blur.

My dialogues with Nina have influenced this integration of theory and practice. Working with Nina has given me a greater respect for precision in language and thought. When I encountered the density and complexity of the texts we read, it intimidated and repulsed me. I have learned to deepen my analyses and to read for a more precise understanding. For instance, I was somewhat overwhelmed and intimidated by Bhabha's writing. However, on the second reading, the language drew me in. I was no longer just reading what Bhabha thought but was making meaning of conceptual threads such as "invisibility" or "evil eye" or "others as watchers" in understanding the construction of "otherness." Gradually, I found myself pulling out these threads in other readings and relating them to my own teaching. Today, I recognize that my students' astute perception of injustices is a reflection of the uncanny ability of those who have been "othered" to be watchers, able to see inequities clearly. My own *conscientização* relocates me on the margins of the teaching collectivity and opens up avenues for arriving at more just, critically self-reflexive pedagogical practices. I struggle with the idea of making my own writing as dense and complex as the ICC readings for fear of discouraging teachers from reading my work. However, I know that the work I have put into understanding these texts has been critical in helping me bridge and develop my own theory and practice.

Teaching, Theory, and Nina's Re-Visioning of the Self

Yes, it is a challenge to balance working toward change and, simultaneously, functioning within extant realities. According to Anzaldúa (1987), one has to cope with the *choque*, the clash of cultures, when one situates oneself on "both shores at once" (78). Of course, we gain by expanding our repertoires and, ultimately, being able to operate in both realms, thereby bringing theory and practice together. That is the powerful aspect of being a mestiza—it is a self, an identity, a space that one creates to make meaning of and find integrity among the diverging realities one encounters. Furthermore, I find that this theorizing opens up pedagogical practice, enabling dialogue among the particular mestiza identifications of different students and colleagues.

Perhaps the toughest challenge here is accepting that such work makes one "rethink" oneself. Not only do we become uneasily aware of our *implicatedness* in the structures and systems we seek to change, but we then struggle to maintain integrity. Where do I belong? In the realm of theory or of practice? Margins or center? Nonetheless, even as we go through such angst-ridden questioning, having swallowed that red pill, we are sustained by the knowledge that the real answers will emerge out of the recursive process, the "continual creative motion that keeps breaking down the unitary aspect of each new paradigm" (Anzaldúa 1987, 80).

Michelle's Continuing Journey

As I make my own path as "practitioner/theorist," I find that the complexities, contradictions, and *implicatednesses* are all right there—requiring me to unravel continually the tensions that emerge between my practice and my theory.

So, of course, it is not resolved yet because I no longer see resolution as a single, finite goal. Rather, the path to deconstructing marginalization and oppression is the ongoing, recursive praxis, the dialogue between my practice and my theory.

Nina's Continuing Journey

Ditto. Only vice versa.

Notes

1. In the Louisiana French immersion program, anglophone students learn subject content in French. The program is set within a "heritage language context," where teachers use a language other than English that is or was historically spoken by the community.

2. The Indian government created this special classification to label various indigenous populations that have, historically, lived in remote, hilly areas of the country and, therefore, have not been part of the "mainstream."

3. I (Michelle) am a white Lebanese American woman who is feeling less and less white in current times.

References

Anzaldúa, G. 1987. *Borderlands/La Frontera: The new mestiza.* San Francisco: Aunt Lute.

Asher, N. 2001. Beyond "cool" and "hip": Engaging the question of research and writing as academic Self—woman of color Other. *International Journal of Qualitative Studies in Education* 14(1): 1–12.

———. 2002. (En)gendering a hybrid consciousness. *Journal of Curriculum Theorizing* 18(4): 81–92.

———. 2003. At the intersections: A postcolonialist woman of color considers Western feminism. *Social Education* 67(1): 47–50.

Bhabha, H. 1994. *The location of culture.* New York: Routledge.

Britzman, D. 1997. The tangles of implication. *International Journal of Qualitative Studies in Education* 10(1): 31–37.

Collins, P. 1991. Learning from the outsider within: The sociological significance of black feminist thought. In *Beyond methodology: Feminist scholarship as lived research,* edited by M. M. Fonow and J. A. Cook. Bloomington: Indiana University Press, 35–59.

Freire, P. 1998. *Pedagogy of the oppressed.* New York: Continuum.

hooks, b. 1990. *Yearning: Race, gender, and cultural politics.* Boston: South End Press.

———. 1994. *Teaching to transgress: Education as the practice of freedom.* New York: Routledge.

Kumashiro, K. 2000. Toward a theory of anti-oppressive education. *Review of Educational Research* 70(1): 25–53.

Mooney, R. 1975. Prelude. In *Curriculum theorizing: The reconceptualists,* edited by W. Pinar. Berkeley, Calif.: McCutchan, 173–74.

Pratt, M. B. 1984. Identity: Skin, blood, heart. In *Yours in struggle: Three feminist perspectives on anti-semitism and racism,* edited by E. Bulkin, M. B. Pratt, and B. Smith. Brooklyn, N.Y.: Long Haul, 11–63.

Sleeter, C. 1993. How white teachers construct race. In *Race, identity, and representation in education,* edited by C. McCarthy and W. Crichlow. New York: Routledge, 157–71.

Villenas, S. 1996. The colonizer/colonized Chicana ethnographer: Identity, marginalization, and co-optation in the field. *Harvard Educational Review* 66(4): 711–31.

Wachowski, L., and A. Wachowski (writers and directors). 1999. *The Matrix* [film]. (Available from Warner Bros. Studios, 4000 Warner Boulevard, Burbank, CA 91522.)

A Contemporary Praxis of Collaboration 10

MARILYN DOERR, PENNSYLVANIA STATE UNIVERSITY
J. DAN MARSHALL, PENNSYLVANIA STATE UNIVERSITY

Most of the chapters in this volume, addressing issues of public moral responsibility, concern collaborations between practitioners and professors, the latter involved in situ with the teacher's project. Together, they meet, huddled over tables laden with paper and cold coffee, dissecting what has happened or might happen, making judgments about how the project is going. But that is not how my (Marilyn's) work progressed. In my project, I am both practitioner and professor, constructing my theory as I engage my data. Yet to say that I do or could do this in solitude would be wrong. While I do not have a fellow professor joining me at the table in my high school science classroom, I, too, am collaborating—just differently.

How does my story on collaboration begin? Three people prove more or less central to my story: Joe Kincheloe in New York, Dan Marshall in Pennsylvania, and Bill Pinar in Louisiana, three professors of education who befriended me in different ways.

While working on my doctorate, I took several courses from Joe Kincheloe. I liked the way Joe ran a class, and I particularly liked the books he chose for us to read. In one of these courses, I was introduced to *Autobiography, Politics, and Sexuality* (Pinar 1994). During that same semester, I received word from the school where I teach that I was to plan a new course in ecology for the following autumn, a senior elective that would make use of our large, wooded campus. While reading Pinar's book, I was introduced to *currere*, and a lightning bolt hit me; I saw the link between *currere* and my new class. Wanting some way of emotionally connecting my students to the environment, I thought Pinar might have just what I needed.

I sat down almost immediately after finishing that book and wrote briefly about how *currere* could fit my ecology course syllabus.

That summer, in another doctoral course, I had to devise a series of lesson plans and assessments. I fleshed out *currere*, feeling even more excited that this idea might really work. I had talked to Kincheloe about different ways *currere* had been used in the past, but he was not aware of actual classroom situations in which this concept had been tried to any extent. Encouraging me to play with the idea, he reminded me of Pinar's genius and what he, Joe, thought was a strong philosophical connection between what Pinar and I thought schools should be.

Dan Marshall was my thesis adviser, though not my first choice. I first met Dan in a course he taught on curriculum history. We, too, shared many ideas about schools. He and I would meet and talk periodically. I eventually asked Dan to be on my dissertation committee, and when my adviser left the institution, I convinced Dan to become my new adviser. He was reluctant to do so because he knew little about the science aspect of my thesis, but knowing we could work together, he agreed.

It was Dan who introduced me to *Toward a Poor Curriculum*, the book in which Bill Pinar and Madeleine Grumet (1976) explore their use of *currere*. I did not even know this book existed. I had not yet seen it referenced in the literature, and it had long been out of print. The university library had no copies on record. After several months of trying to locate it, I was about to give up when Dan suggested that I e-mail Bill about securing a copy. Bill and I had a short cyberspace exchange, and within days I found a copy of *Toward a Poor Curriculum* in my mailbox—his gift to me.

Looking back, this was a kind of "staging" time for our collaboration that would follow. As I (Dan) recall, Marilyn spent her year in residency at Penn State exploring ideas, connecting with faculty members, taking courses, and completing her comprehensive exams. By the time she returned to Cleveland, she had successfully presented a dissertation proposal to explore currere *in her ecology classroom (Doerr 2000).*

Marilyn had not been gone a year before her thesis adviser left Penn State and I assumed that role. Not long after that, Joe Kincheloe was gone to New York. The challenging work of our collaboration had begun. How have the four of us worked together these past five years— Marilyn in Ohio, Joe in New York, Dan in Pennsylvania, Bill in Louisiana—with an idea that each of us was invested in differently?

What is this idea of *currere* and of my adaptation, what I call the environmental autobiography, or EA? *Currere* was one outgrowth of the reconceptualization approach to curriculum begun in the mid-1970s. Pinar developed the concept to help beginning teachers think about how they wanted to teach and what they could do to "reconceptualize" their ideas about what good teaching meant. *Currere* focuses on the educational experience of the individual as reported by the individual; it seeks to describe what the individual her- or himself makes of behaviors. *Currere* is grounded in phenomenology and existentialism and the works of Carl Jung and of R. D. Laing. Pinar characterized the method with the following four steps: the method is 1) regressive, involving description of one's intellectual biography; 2) progressive, involving a description of one's imagined future; 3) analytic, calling for a psychoanalysis of one's phenomenologically described past, present, and future; and 4) synthetic, totalizing the fragments of experience and placing this integrated understanding of individual experience into a large political and cultural web (Pinar 1975, 424). How is it possible, Pinar questioned, for students to experience continuity in educational experience where so often we experience discontinuity and disjointedness? If he could get beginning teachers to internalize this question and to see where it may have worked or not worked in their lives, maybe they would rethink curriculum and work toward making schooling a cohesive whole.

I had a similar goal. How could I get my ecology students to see that they were part of a whole—part of a fragile planet that needed to be treated respectfully? If I could get them to see what an important role the environment had played in their lives, maybe they could then move to thinking about what they could do to ensure that the environment would be around for succeeding generations.

The EA is my adaptation of *currere.* The students and I worked over a four-month period, one stage each month. I told them they would be writing an autobiography about their experiences with the environment in the past, the present, and the future (Doerr 2004).

Currere moved my students from "I know" to "I care" to "I want to do something about this." Overpopulation, the exhaustion of energy resources, the pollution of the biosphere, the threat of nuclear weapons, the dehumanizing structures in technology, and the widening gap between rich and poor share a complex causality and a common cause: an indifference to human values. Values of honesty, integrity, cooperation, responsibility, justice, caring, self-fulfillment, and joy—these are values that become moral imperatives in a global world. Through *currere*, students become aware of their perceived connectedness to others. They begin to explore how human values fit into their lives and the degree of importance of these values.

I am fortunate to teach in a private school. I have the freedom to experiment. I am trusted and respected to add to, subtract from, and reconfigure my curriculum. *Currere* takes time—protracted time in order to work its magic. I was able to teach the basic ecology concepts the course demanded, but I needed to take some classroom time for *currere*. Since the bulk of the students' writings were done outside class, we shared writings and talked over the nuances of the various stages in class. Outside class, I spent long hours every eight school days or so reading approximately thirty EAs and responding in writing to the new work. At the end, I reread everyone's entire EA and wrote an extensive letter to each student.

Currere can be successful only if there is a prepared classroom environment. There must be an expectation of group discussion where students listen and respect others' ideas. There must be an atmosphere of safety where students can say what they want (within boundaries) and not worry that conversation will leave the classroom. The teacher must be prepared to sit back and let the group take over, yet be organized to give feedback in a timely manner.

The extra time and the extra effort are well worth it. The cohesiveness the class develops in the shared experience of *currere* is amazing. There is a vitality to *currere*—it has a "mind" of its own—and once put into play, the practitioner sits back and watches where this mind will lead.

My first experience with the mind of *currere* was disconcerting, and I did not quite know what to make of it. I was excited, the students were excited, but I was not sure why. It was in the collaboration with my three companions that I began to deconstruct this process; eventually, we learned how to better read the mind of *currere*.

Historically, collaboration often has been perceived negatively. Enemies collaborate; shifting coalitions exist to collaborate on some cause that for a short time they all believe in. Some even find today's scientists collaborating to prevent information from reaching the public. How have we in the academy evolved our definition of collaboration? That is the operative word—"evolved." Collaboration is one of those words that should not be defined too narrowly. We suggest this definition: collaboration is two or more people coming together intellectually to work through a problem. Where, why, and how it is done varies significantly.

Just as the teacher–student relationship involves both parties both teaching and learning, collaboration between consenting adults situates all parties on equal degrees of latitude. With today's Internet prevalence, it is not uncommon to find long discussions, organizations of meetings and conferences, and shared data collection taking place in cyberspace. Few could argue that this technology has allowed for some collaborations that, prior to the Internet, almost never took place.

The praxis of our collaboration changed for me over the five-year span of my project. Qualitative researchers often write about the need for group processing—that is, finding someone with whom to discuss one's research and analytic thinking. Yet I was pretty much unable to do this in my immediate locale. No colleague in my high school science department was even remotely interested. My method of *currere* was (and is) considered on the fringe. Once I actually began the ecology course, Dan and Bill became my "virtual" collaborators in my attempt to "practice" the theory.

Dan and I became collaborative theorizers. The attractiveness of this approach, Lather (1991) says, is that "all participants, within time constraints, are allowed a role in negotiating the final meanings of the research" (58). Because Dan and I looked at the data from such different directions, we looked uniquely. Bill, on the other hand, was more the "heart" of our collaboration. I needed him to tell me that in my adaptation I had not lost the initial sense of *currere*. Both would help me negotiate the final meanings of my research.

I also needed Dan and Bill to see the significance of my sometimes unsophisticated, sometimes highly sophisticated writings. Although several fellow teachers knew of the nature and extent of these writings and how involved students were with the work (Doerr and Marshall 2002), the only response I ever got from my teacher colleagues was a negative one. Indeed, during the fourth year of my project, I was told that I could no longer make the "product" of our EA (a lengthy, autobiographical paper) due just before exams. It was deemed "against school policy" to have such a major assignment due right around exam time. Despite my efforts to convince administrators that this was not a "normal" assignment, they would not reconsider. Sometimes, I think that without Bill and Dan I might not continue with the EA. In many ways they serve as buoys, reminding me of the importance of what I am trying to accomplish.

In June 2002, I presented a paper at a conference in New York City to a group of educators, many of whom I thought would not be interested in this radical technique for science teaching. Though my audience was small, at the end an administrator said to me, "Hang in there, the work you are doing is so important." I also get responses from parents, such as this one, that lift my spirits and keep me going:

> Your ecology class and your commitment to the environment has had such an impact on [my son] and the further development of a lifelong ambition to make this a better planet; I know your lessons will go with him through college and beyond. The work you do . . . and your commitment to doing what is right should be commended. You have made a lasting impression on [my son], and you've played a very instrumental role in the path he has chosen to take into adulthood. I can never thank you enough for all that you have given my son; I am confident that your relationship with him will make him a better man. (personal correspondence with author, July 11, 2002)

This mother, though, could not understand the EA project in the way I did, the way Dan did, or, in particular, the way Bill did. She, too, might have told me to "hang in there," but she simply could not know how larger eco-logical issues were embedded in the particulars of her son's everyday life. She did not (or could not) read and analyze her son's writings; she was too close to the subject. The distance Dan and Bill brought to my original analyses was imperative for a meaningful collaboration. Lather (1991, 87) says there is a "messy complexity" to lived experience. It was that original "mess" they helped me through.

What Marilyn is too polite to say here is that I (Dan) was instrumental in creating and maintaining our particular "mess." Like Marilyn's assessment of the mother of whom she speaks, I was convinced that Marilyn herself was too close to the project to see currere's larger theoretical and methodological issues relative to her dissertation research—issues that were deeply embedded in her everyday interaction with this young man. Collaboration, espe-cially between doctoral students and their dissertation advisers, is "messy" indeed, and I was seriously concerned that Marilyn would become lost amidst her mess of data.

With the clarity of hindsight and the special reflective opportunity offered by a project such as this, I have learned that the doctoral dissertation should be a true collaboration between stu-dent and adviser—a collaboration in which both must accept roles of novice and expert, learner and teacher. Worried about Marilyn's frameworks and constructions, I completely missed her quiet and respectful efforts to help me see what she was trying to accomplish. Thanks to her, I am a better learner within these academically intense and intimate relationships.

Like ours, a true collaboration should be a mutually educative experience: I learn from Bill and Dan, and they learn from me. We stay open to each other's response to a story, a paragraph, and try to read each other critically. But this is not always easy. I tend to get upset and remind Dan that he is not the one working with these students every day, dealing with the management of the class, but even as I say or write these words, I know I am overreacting. When I eventually calm down, I try to look at what about his response makes me fly off the handle or depresses me. For example, while I was writing my thesis, Dan did not want me to write about fifty different students. He felt it was sufficient to pick a few cases and build my story from there. I, who knew these students and in many cases had worked with some of them over several years, could not even begin to think about absenting anyone from the presented data. I also felt it was important to show writings from everyone to get an idea of the mix of tales, to see that even at age eighteen there was a large disparity in how some of them perceived their "false consciousness." But if Dan had not continued to question me about that decision—which I made early on and never wavered from—I know I would not have critically looked at my decision.

Husserl (1970), the father of phenomenology, says that we can know what we experience only by attending to perceptions and meanings that awaken our conscious awareness. We have to be conscious of the experience. When the students do their regression, they sometimes write stories remembered on a subconscious level. Possibly they were too young; possibly their parents or grandparents remind them of an experience. The EA helps bring consciousness to the lived experience. In their descriptions, explications, and interpretations of the experience, students relive the story. Patton (1990) writes that we "focus on how we put together the phenomena we experience in such a way as to make sense of the world and, in so doing, develop a worldview. There is no separate (or objective) reality for people" (69). It is one of the myriad interesting parts of regression to watch that interpretation sometimes change for a late adolescent from what it was when actually experienced, say, as an eight-year-old or an early adolescent. Sometimes it is difficult for the student not to "spin" the story.

This "interpretive turn" was an area in which Dan's and Bill's collaboration with my project proved especially helpful. As readers, they were taking different viewpoints. Dan was not particularly interested in hearing the student's background for his stories, whereas Bill felt the background was helpful for him in making sense of the student's writing. I could not get beyond the need to have the reader understand the student in a fuller way. What sense would the reader make of the student by reading only a few paragraphs? I had worked with these students daily, some of them over a period of two or three years. What I had to keep reminding myself was that neither Bill nor Dan had ever set foot in my classroom, met any of these students, or seen the class in session. Nothing anchored their interpretations of what I was giving them. At first I found this frustrating, though as time went on I realized this was an advantage. First, all my other readers would find themselves in exactly the same position as Bill and Dan. Second, I could not rely on my intuitive response to the students. I knew my collaborators could question me about any of these students or any of their writings, and I had to be prepared to give a cogent reason for writing what I did. Their long-distance collaboration forced me to be more precise in my writing and to think more deeply about my perceptions of each student.

I came to value that they were coming from different positions. I kept finding myself leaning toward reading Bill's responses rather than Dan's because I could not imagine writing about these students differently. Bill would respond to individual students, and I could tell he was reading each student's stories carefully. I liked that; I wanted him to know and like my students as I did. I wanted him to understand their intensity and seriousness as they went about this work, and I especially wanted him to feel their enthusiasm and sense of accomplishment. Because he had been frustrated in the past with bringing *currere* into the classroom, I wanted him to be excited. It was, after all, Bill Pinar who conceived of this amazing method. He was the inventor; I was the "manufacturer."

And I was the thesis adviser who believed that this role carried certain responsibilities that frequently seemed to put Marilyn and me at odds with each other. I was not pleased with her decision to include data from so many students in her dissertation and found myself skimming through the pages of description and analysis looking for patterns and representations of the theoretical principles and tenets of currere. *My feedback tended to address the historical and philosophical aspects of her work at the expense of individual students' personal epiphanies. I needed an organizational scheme for her presentations that made sense to me. And we disagreed about these issues until the day of her successful dissertation defense.*

Slowly, behind all this, her passion for these students' stories began to emerge for me. We would talk for long periods about her struggle to understand these tales, and eventually I came to see their importance to her as a complex data set that required her interpretations. With Marilyn's patient and persistent support, I slowly realized that my fixation on her work as a doctoral student clouded my ability to even see, let alone understand and appreciate, her as a teacher. She saw lives; I saw data.

Marilyn remembers distinctly the day I announced that I was beginning to realize the "power" of currere. *It was an expression she used many times after that. "There is a power in* currere," *Marilyn would write, a power to change the world, to make people better, to make environments better. Introducing* currere *to these ecology students was Marilyn's attempt to encourage young people to realize their deepest affiliations with natural surroundings. As she labored to make sense of how students articulated their ecological selves, I labored to get her to accept my suggestions for channeling her analytical and interpretive efforts. She wanted students to see that they can change the world; I, the fool, wanted only to change Marilyn's mind.*

Beyond the students' phenomenological experiences lies my phenomenology of using *currere* with them. My considerable personal experience has led to an intense interest in understanding what that means for us all. Each year my understanding deepens as I look at how my students use *currere*, how I present *currere* to them, and how *currere* itself has its own impetus. What does it mean for my students to have this experience; what will it mean for them in the future? What can it mean for the planet?

While drawn to Lather's (1991) discussion of catalytic validity, I remain uncomfortable with the notion in the context of this project. I am reluctant to let students read others' EA segments unless a student initiates such readings. And while I continually discuss possible meanings of stories with their creators, I never discuss the entire body of data or what I think the data mean, in totality, with them. Since each student has a unique, private experience with the EA, I respect that privacy. Yet I often think about the possibility that this is and was a mistake. These doubts persist because the collaborative theorizing I have done with Bill and Dan has provided so much support to my work.

And now, three years later (five years after the initiation of *currere* in my classroom), Bill Pinar, Dan Marshall, and I continue to collaborate around my project, though now our shared time is spent exchanging book and journal manuscripts instead of my dissertation chapters. We collaborate less often, but we still give support and counsel if needed.

Collaboration, in our case, involves layers of respect—among and between Marilyn, Bill, and Dan and Marilyn's ecology students—and, in our collaboration around *currere*, respect for the environment. When it works, none of us loses our identity, our autonomy. And at the same time, we become better, we become more. In our contemporary praxis of collaboration, the whole is truly greater than the sum of its parts.

References

Doerr, M. 2000. A high school ecology curriculum employing *currere*: A critical postmodern approach to pedagogy. Ph.D. diss., Pennsylvania State University.

———. 2004. *Currere and the environmental autobiography: A phenomenological approach to the teaching of ecology.* New York: Peter Lang.

Doerr, M., and J. Marshall. 2002. Teaching "from the middle": Bringing *currere* to high school ecology studies. *Scholar Practitioner Quarterly* 1(2): 7–23.

Husserl, E. 1970. *The crisis of European sciences and transcendental phenomenology.* Translated by D. Carr. Evanston, Ill.: Northwestern University Press.

Lather, P. 1991. *Getting smart: Feminist research and pedagogy with/in the postmodern.* New York: Routledge.

Patton, M. 1990. *Qualitative evaluation and research methods.* Newbury Park, Calif.: Sage.

Pinar, W. 1975. *Curriculum theorizing: The reconceptualists.* Berkeley, Calif.: McCutchan.

———. 1994. *Autobiography, politics, and sexuality: Essays in curriculum theory, 1972–1992.* New York: Peter Lang.

Pinar, W., and M. Grumet. 1976. *Toward a poor curriculum.* Dubuque, Iowa: Kendall/Hunt.

The Problem of the Public I I

WILLIAM F. PINAR, LOUISIANA STATE UNIVERSITY

[T]he need for a public moral voice and schooling for social justice has never been more urgent or seldom less apparent.

—JAMES T. SEARS (CHAPTER 1 IN THIS VOLUME, 4)

The essential need . . . is the improvement of the methods and conditions of debate, discussion and persuasion. That is the *problem of the public.*

—JOHN DEWEY (1991, 208)

As James Sears asserts, never has the need for reconstructing the public moral sphere in the United States been more urgent than it is today. Never, he suggests, has it been less apparent. "[I]f . . . the citizen [is] nothing but a capital resource, with education nothing more than job training," David G. Smith (2003) asks, what serves "to anchor the teaching profession and provide it with public moral authority?" (296). Sears's observation and Smith's question express the urgency of the problem of the public in the present historical moment.

To participate in the conversation conducted in this collection, I turn to John Dewey's (1991) *The Public and Its Problems.* In Dewey's estimation, the "essential need" in the formation of the public sphere has two elements: the methods and conditions of debate, discussion, and persuasion. During the past thirty years, the field of curriculum studies has come far in elaborating the methods for improving debate, discussion, and persuasion. From theatre as pedagogy and environmental autobiography to transformative curriculum leadership, artistic education, and a curriculum of care, the chapters in this volume document that curriculum workers understand a wide range of methods that enable us to participate in curriculum understood as "complicated conversation."

Yet, as Dewey appreciated, the problem of the public includes the improvement not only of our methods but also of the conditions of debate, discussion, and persuasion. As we are painfully aware, the conditions enabling "curriculum as complicated conversation" have deteriorated dramatically during the past forty years. What is at stake in right-wing reform—which has converted the school into a business, focused on the "bottom line" (standardized test scores)—is the political and intellectual control of the curriculum, that is, what teachers are permitted to teach and what children are permitted to study. Especially from the 1960s (starting with the 1964 Barry Goldwater campaign), the right wing in the United States has appreciated that its political ascendancy depends on controlling how and what Americans think.

The school, remodeled as a knowledge-and-skill factory (or now, in a presumably postindustrial economy, the school as corporation, wherein teachers are "managers" of students' "learning") creates profoundly anti-intellectual conditions in the schools, conditions that foreclose debate, discussion, and persuasion. Especially since September 11, 2001, the right wing has employed the terrorist threat to manipulate public opinion, suppress dissent, and move the nation far to the right. Written almost eighty years ago, also during a decade of right-wing ascendancy, Dewey (1991) observed, "The creation of political unity has also promoted social and intellectual uniformity, a standardization favorable to mediocrity. Opinion has been regimented as well as outward behavior" (115). Standardization, through the apparently commonsensical insistence on "standards" and "accountability," stifles not only dissent but also creativity, individuality, indeed, subjectivity itself. Education disappears, replaced by political socialization.

In this volume, contributors such as Joanne M. Arhar and Rebecca McElfresh articulate how the problem of the public, conceived as that of reconstructing curriculum as a public moral enterprise, is made nearly impossible when government itself acts to control debate and dialogue. Our academic—intellectual—freedom to teach the curriculum and devise those means by which to assess its study have been usurped by politicians in the name of "accountability." As Linda McNeil (2000) has pointed out, "[t]he conservative transformation of American public education [has occurred] through the use of technicist forms of power" (7). To put the matter bluntly, "accountability" is the face of fascism in the United States today.

The politically enforced estrangement between education professors and schoolteachers—accomplished by the 1960s national curriculum reform movement—has been misinterpreted by some as a chosen estrangement (Brooks 2001; Wraga 1999). The severance of curriculum scholars from active participation in curriculum development has not only *not* been chosen, it has been contested by many curriculum workers, including several whose work appears in this volume. This very contestation underscores the fact that our position is not chosen but forced on us and, indeed, resisted. Chapter 6, by Rosemary Gornik, James Henderson, and Michelle D. Thomas, for instance, is an eloquent statement of professional commitment that simultaneously discloses lost influence: "[W]e passionately work to develop a public trust for our professional judgment with colleagues, community members, and politicians" (59). As engaging as this project was for those who participated, when the money was gone, school personnel declined to participate. The same exodus occurred in the Theatre as Pedagogy project led by Morna McDermott, Toby Daspit, and Kevin Dodd (chapter 7). In neither instance was the "method" (to use Dewey's term) employed to blame; it was the "conditions" in which methods were practiced that undermined the project. Once financial incentives (conditions in Dewey's formulation) were removed, school personnel departed.

Despite unfavorable conditions, the "curriculum and pedagogy" movement in U.S. curriculum studies is dedicated to reconstructing the public moral sphere in education, as its conferences and proceedings indicate (Allen et al. 2003; Poetter et al. 2002; Sloan and Sears 2001).[1] Having attended two of these conferences, it is clear to me that participants' understanding of "methods"—to use again Dewey's conceptualization of the problem of the public—is sophisticated. By the use of "town meetings," in the inclusion of school personnel and in numerous innovative arts-based presentations, it is obvious that conference participants appreciate what methods are required to conduct "curriculum work as a public moral enterprise."

Nonetheless, there are a few who appear to confuse "conditions" with "methods" and assume that "if we build it, they will come." In this view, the problem of the public seems a simple matter of how *we* scholars have positioned ourselves. In a curiously patrician image, Barbara Brodhagen and Michael W. Apple (chapter 3) suggest that we scholars have chosen to view the school from "the balcony." While there may be curriculum scholars who look down on the schools, few of us enjoy an elevated position in the present historical moment. Severed from the school curriculum, disdained by too many colleagues in faculties of arts and sciences,[2] and exploited even by our own administrators, the university is itself being corporatized as education professors are being "deintellectualized." The curriculum content of teacher education courses is being increasingly specified by government and accrediting agencies. Indeed, those of us located in the university face the same fate as our colleagues located in the schools—no elevated position to be sure.

Our severance from schools was never chosen, and certainly it was never an expression of haughtiness on the part of curriculum scholars, as if we preferred peering from the balcony rather than "dancing" directly with our school colleagues on a horizontal floor of collaboration.[3] In the conclusion to *Understanding Curriculum* (Pinar et al. 1995), my colleagues and I suggested that

> instead of wringing our hands over lost influence in the schools . . . we might commit ourselves to understanding what curriculum is, has been, and might be. It bears repeating that this does not mean fleeing from "practice," turning our backs on teachers, pretending to be like arts and sciences professors, as many educational foundations professors have pretended in the past. We curriculum theorists must still offer friendship and colleagueship to teachers; we must offer teachers our expertise as they request (and as circumstances permit it to be offered and to be accepted). (851)

Structural *conditions* imposed by others, not our *methods*, split us from the schools.

What has changed since we wrote that paragraph ten years ago? Today politicians are scapegoating schoolteachers more intensely than ever before, and education professors are also being positioned as culprits in the right-wing assault on public education in the United States. According to U.S.

Secretary of Education Rod Paige (2002), the courses we teach are only "hurdles" tripping up hordes of talented college graduates who would otherwise enthusiastically enter the teaching profession. Moreover, we are told that there is "empirical" evidence that demonstrates that teachers who have been spared education course work are more successful at raising their students' test scores than teachers who have not. This "business" model of education—where the bottom line (standardized test scores) is all that matters—is now enforced by federal legislation and encouraged by presumably professional organizations, such as the American Association of Colleges for Teacher Education and the National Council for Accreditation of Teacher Education (see Pinar 2004).

Under such conditions, it is dangerously delusional to assume that "if we build it they will come." What can we do? "Leaving safe harbors" (Carlson 2002) and "teaching convictions" (Slattery and Rapp 2002) underscore the performative character of our methods for reconstructing the classroom as a public moral enterprise. In certain schools, conditions permit innovative methods; Marilyn Doerr (chapter 10) enjoys sufficient academic freedom to experiment with the curriculum of her secondary school course. She acknowledges, "I am fortunate to teach in a private school. I have the freedom to experiment. I am trusted and respected to add to, subtract from, and reconfigure my curriculum" (112).

Such academic—intellectual—freedom is the prerequisite *condition* to reconstructing the public moral sphere in curriculum and teaching. Only when that condition is present can sophisticated scholars (such as Rubén A. Gaztambide-Fernández) and teachers (such as Anne R. Clark) engage in a "conversation regarding the ways in which curriculum theory could inform the particular challenges confronted by BAA [Boston Arts Academy] faculty" (chapter 5, 50), enabling high school faculty to "support student artists as cultural workers contributing to a vibrant democratic society" (56). Reminiscent of the work of William Heard Kilpatrick, the capstone project that Clark and Gaztambide-Fernández describe seems to me an exciting curriculum innovation connecting the social with the subjective through academic knowledge and, in so doing, reconstructing the public moral sphere in curriculum and teaching.

Despite unfavorable conditions, there remain innovative teacher education programs, as the collaboration between Susan Finley and Jason Adams (chapter 8) suggests. Like a box on a sidewalk, "theory" can function as a refuge, fragile but mobile: "[T]heory," Finley comments, "forms a space for Jason to shape his teaching" (85). The ongoing conversation evident in the Finley–Adams collaboration need not require physical proximity, as the transpacific collaboration between Mina Kim and Soo Ryeon Lee (chapter 4) implies. It is crystal clear from this collection that we know "methods" for reconstructing the classroom into a public moral sphere, even during a historical moment when "conditions" make such intellectual and pedagogical labor excruciatingly difficult, even dangerous.

What can be done about these anti-intellectual, antieducational "conditions"? As Sears (chapter 1) observes, reconstructing the classroom as a public moral sphere is not enough: "Today, curriculum workers must advocate *within* the public square for a moral education in which curriculum and pedagogy for human dignity, social and economic justice, spiritual enlightenment, and peace and sustainability are the new standards of excellence" (5; emphasis in the original). How might we organize such advocacy? How might we change the conditions in which we employ our methods?

Tom Barone's (2000) endorsement of fiction as one way of portraying the lived realities of teaching to the public and to their legislative representatives remains one important answer to that question. Teacher unions could become useful by funding a national television campaign—featuring, perhaps, movie and athletic icons to attract viewers' attention—explaining (for starters) that education is not a business. Scholarly organizations such as the American Educational Research Association could establish an Office of Public Education funded to support selected scholars' and teachers' talks to taxpayers at, say, public libraries across the nation, answering questions, explaining in everyday language what we know already theoretically.

The construction of a public moral sphere in the United States is a struggle to educate the American public. That is, of course, the project of "public education." Today it requires us to teach not only our students but also their parents, our neighbors, and anyone who will listen. By whatever means, we must continue teaching after the bell rings and students depart our classrooms. Alone and together, we can "teach for America." This volume represents an important lesson.

Notes

1. For more information on the Curriculum and Pedagogy Conference, see www.ed.asu.edu/candp/main.html (accessed January 14, 2004).

2. The closing of the University of Chicago's Department of Education is a recent and visible example of our politically vulnerable situation in the university. For others, see Pinar (2004), chap. 7, sec. I.

3. In other countries, "conditions" differ from ours (Pinar 2003; Trueit et al. 2003).

References

Allen, L., D. A. Breault, D. Cartner, C. Chargois, R. A. Gaztambide-Fernández, M. Hayes, K. Krasny, and B. Setser, eds. 2003. *Democratic curriculum. Theory and practice: Retrieving public spaces.* Troy, N.Y.: Educators International Press.

Barone, T. 2000. *Aesthetics, politics, and educational inquiry.* New York: Peter Lang.

Brooks, N. 2001. Paul Klohr and the second wave. In *Democratic curriculum theory and practice: Retrieving public spaces,* edited by K. Sloan and J. T. Sears. Troy, N.Y.: Educators International Press, 49–65.

Carlson, D. 2002. *Leaving safe harbors: Toward a new progressivism in American education and public life.* New York: Routledge.

Dewey, J. 1991. *The public and its problems.* Athens: Ohio University Press.

McNeil, L. M. 2000. *Contradictions of school reform: Educational costs of standardized testing.* New York: Routledge.

Paige, R. 2002. *Meeting the highly qualified teachers challenge: The Secretary's annual report on teacher quality.* Washington, D.C.: U.S. Department of Education, Office of Postsecondary Education.

Pinar, W. F., ed. 2003. *International handbook of curriculum research.* Mahwah, N.J.: Lawrence Erlbaum Associates.

———. 2004. *What is curriculum theory?* Mahwah, N.J.: Lawrence Erlbaum Associates.

Pinar, W. F., W. M. Reynolds, P. Slattery, and P. M. Taubman. 1995. *Understanding curriculum: An introduction to historical and contemporary curriculum discourses.* New York: Peter Lang.

Poetter, T. S., C. Haerr, M. Hayes, C. Higgins, and K. Wilson Baptist, eds. 2002. *In(ex)clusion: (Re)visioning the democratic ideal.* Troy, N.Y.: Educators International Press.

Slattery, P., and D. Rapp. 2002. *Ethics and the foundations of education: Teaching convictions in a postmodern world.* Boston: Allyn & Bacon.

Sloan, K., and J. T. Sears, eds. 2001. *Democratic curriculum theory and practice: Retrieving public spaces.* Troy, N.Y.: Educators International Press.

Smith, D. G. 2003. The specific challenges of globalization for teaching . . . and vice versa. In *The internationalization of curriculum studies,* edited by D. Trueit, W. E. Doll Jr., H. Wang, and W. F. Pinar. New York: Peter Lang, 293–318.

Trueit, D., W. Doll Jr., H. Wang, and W. F. Pinar, eds. 2003. *The internationalization of curriculum studies.* New York: Peter Lang.

Wraga, W. G. 1999. Extracting sun-beams out of cucumbers: The retreat from practice in reconceptualized curriculum studies. *Educational Researcher* 28: 4–13.

Index

About the Contributors

Jason Adams is a recent graduate of the Master's in Teaching program at Washington State University, Vancouver. Currently, he is seeking employment in early elementary education in Washington and Oregon school districts in the Portland metropolitan area.

Michael W. Apple is the John Bascom Professor of Curriculum and Instruction and Educational Policy Studies at the University of Wisconsin, Madison. Among his most recent books are *Educating the "Right" Way* and *The State and the Politics of Knowledge*.

Joanne M. Arhar is an associate professor of curriculum and instruction and coordinator of middle childhood education at Kent State University. She has been a classroom teacher, school administrator, and staff development specialist prior to completing her doctoral work at the University of Cincinnati. Her areas of interest include middle-level teacher education, action research, and the organization of middle-level schools.

Nina Asher is an assistant professor in the Department of Curriculum and Instruction at Louisiana State University, Baton Rouge. Her scholarship focuses on postcolonial and feminist theory, multiculturalism, and Asian American education.

Barbara Brodhagen is the learning coordinator at the Sherman Middle School in Madison, Wisconsin. For most of her career, she has been a classroom teacher, but she has also held a variety of positions in public education in Wisconsin and New York state. She is coauthor with James Beane of "Teaching in Middle Schools" in the *Handbook of Research on Teaching*, edited by Virginia Richardson, and with Michael Apple of "The Situation Made Us Special" in *Democratic Schools*, edited by Michael Apple and James Beane.

Anne R. Clark is the curriculum coordinator and a humanities/special education teacher at Boston Arts Academy. She received her A.B. from Harvard College and her master's in English and American literature from the University of Wisconsin, Madison, where she did doctoral work in secondary literacy theory and instruction. Prior to the Boston Arts Academy, she taught writing, cultural studies, and literature at the University of Wisconsin. She also worked with the Boston Annenberg Challenge, the Boston Public Schools' reform initiative, on high school curriculum, school organization, and professional development. She holds certification in English at the secondary level and is pending principal and special education certifications.

Toby Daspit is assistant professor in the College of Education at Western Michigan University. He is the coeditor of *Popular Culture and Critical Pedagogy* and the forthcoming *Science Fiction Curriculum, Cyborg Teachers, and Youth Culture(s)*.

Kevin Dodd, a theater artist/educator, received a B.A. from Western Michigan University in educational theater and has trained with international artists such as Anne Bogart and the S.I.T.I. Company in New York, Graffiti Youth Theatre in Ireland, and Headlines Theatre in British Columbia. Currently, Dodd works with university and community health education agencies on the development of peer education theater programs. He is the founder and director of Shifting Forms, an applied theater company that focuses on creating original work with an ensemble and theater for social change.

Marilyn Doerr is a secondary school science teacher at a private school in Cleveland, Ohio. She teaches astronomy, chemistry, ecology, and human anatomy and physiology. She has also taught middle school science. While earning her Ph.D. in curriculum and instruction at Penn State University, she became interested in phenomenology and has worked on bringing aspects of that philosophy into her science classrooms.

Susan Finley is an assistant professor of social and philosophical foundations, literacy, and research methodology at Washington State University, Vancouver. She bases her pedagogy and inquiry in arts-based approaches to understanding social and cultural issues. Her experiences with displaced youths include working in street schools in Detroit, with street kids and travelers in New Orleans and other urban areas, in tent communities, and with educational programming for unhoused children and their families living in shelters and transitional housing.

Rubén A. Gaztambide-Fernández is an advanced doctoral fellow at the Harvard Graduate School of Education, where he is a Spencer Research Training Grantee and an instructor in education. He is former cochair of the *Harvard Educational Review*, where he also coedited the Popular Culture and Education Special Issue and the reprint collection *Cultural Studies and Education: Perspectives on Theory, Methodology, and Practice*. In addition to working with arts education organizations, his current research focuses on the study of elite schooling. He lives with his wife and daughter in Cambridge, Massachusetts, where they like to dance before going to sleep.

Rosemary Gornik, Ph.D., is the executive director of instruction in the South Euclid-Lyndhurst City Schools in Ohio. She has consulted nationally with schools in the area of teacher development, curriculum development, and strategic planning and has presented at local, state, and national conferences.

Michelle Haj-Broussard is a doctoral candidate in the Department of Curriculum and Instruction at Louisiana State University, Baton Rouge, and a French immersion teacher in the Lafayette Parish School District. Her dissertation focuses on the experiences of African American students in both the French immersion and regular education contexts.

James Henderson is a professor of curriculum at Kent State University. He has specialized in the theory and practice of curriculum leadership in democratic societies. He has authored or coauthored texts on reflective teaching, curriculum leadership, and curriculum wisdom.

Mina Kim is a doctoral student at Indiana University, Bloomington, specializing in early childhood education in the Department of Curriculum and Instruction. She taught preschool and kindergarten in South Korea after she received an M.A. in early childhood education. Her research interests include teacher education reform, critical pedagogy, and qualitative inquiry.

Soo Ryeon Lee is currently teaching kindergarten in South Korea. Since she completed her M.A. in early childhood education at Sungkunkwan University, Seoul, she has been working as a kindergarten teacher for five years. She is particularly interested in peace education, social learning in the classroom, and conflict management.

J. Dan Marshall is a professor in the Department of Curriculum and Instruction and a member of the Educational Leadership program faculty at Penn State University's College of Education. A former elementary and middle school teacher in the United States and Australia, he previously served as a faculty member and associate dean at the National College of Education in Evanston, Illinois. His scholarly and personal interests and activities include home schooling, charter schools, curriculum studies, LGBT issues in education, and teacher education reform.

Morna McDermott received her Ph.D. from University of Virginia in 2000. Her scholarship examines arts-informed construction and representation of data in teacher education. She is currently an assistant professor in the Department of Elementary Education at Towson University, Towson, Maryland. Her work with preservice and in-service teachers includes arts-based approaches to promoting diversity, social justice, and democracy in the classroom. She also serves as an adjunct faculty member for the Lesley University Creative Arts in Learning master's degree program.

Rebecca McElfresh serves as a principal with the Hudson City Schools in Hudson, Ohio. Her experience in public schools includes the roles of elementary classroom teacher, elementary magnet unit teacher for academically talented students, district coordinator of programs for talent development, and elementary school principal. She is a doctoral student in curriculum studies at Kent State University. Her academic interests are in the area of arts-based research, particularly the notion of art making for the process of social change. Her own work with visual art and music informs her academic pursuits.

William F. Pinar teaches curriculum theory at Louisiana State University, where he serves as the St. Bernard Parish Alumni Endowed Professor. He has lectured widely, including Harvard University, McGill University, and the universities of Chicago, Oslo, and Tokyo. He is the founder and now president of the International Association for the Advancement of Curriculum Studies. He is the author of *The Gender of Racial Politics and Violence in America*, the senior author of *Understanding Curriculum*, and the editor of several collections, including *Queer Theory in Education*, *Contemporary Curriculum Discourses*, and the *International Handbook of Curriculum Research*. In the spring of 2000, he received the LSU Distinguished Faculty Award and an AERA Lifetime Achievement Award. Pinar was an English teacher at the Paul D. Schreiber High School in Port Washington, Long Island, New York, from 1969 to 1971.

James T. Sears specializes in research in queer issues in education, curriculum studies, and gay history. He is professor of curriculum studies at the University of South Carolina and the author, coauthor, or editor of fourteen books, including *When Best Doesn't Equal Good*; *Curriculum, Religion, and Public Education*; *Growing Up Gay in the South*; and *Turning Points in Curriculum*. A more detailed biography can be found in *Who's Who in the South and Southwest* and *Contemporary Authors* and at www.jtsears.com.

Michelle D. Thomas serves as an elementary school principal at a private school in the Midwest while pursuing her doctorate at Kent State University. She has presented her work on collaborative inquiry at local, state, and national/international conferences.